ALSO BY ANNIKA GALLOWAY

The Happy Treatment

ISBN: 979-8-218-32939-6

First Edition, 2024

The Waiting Room

A series of short stories by Annika Galloway

We all share the same space, but not the same world.

Azaleas

Annika Galloway

For Grandmother,

whose positivity is always capable of finding a perfect moment.

AZALEAS

Pink azalea,
symbolizing kindness, positivity and
love.

Julie

Fake Flowers

"Oh, this seat's taken," the old man says, as I approach him after leaving the sign-in desk. He places his hand gently on the cold, cheap chair next to him. "I'm waiting for someone."

I don't say anything, as I instead take the seat directly across from him. The cushion on this one seems more worn and the arms of the chair are freezing, but the hospital waiting room is crowded and there aren't many options. I'd much rather sit in the other chair, which is a little more comfortable, but the energy to argue left me long ago. I place my bony elbow on the cold, metal arm of the chair and run my hand through my thin, gray hair.

I hate having to come here so often; it's just a reminder that I'm old, and that things aren't perfect anymore – not like they used to be.

"Julie?"

I blink and look up, startled from my thoughts.

"That's a pretty name," the old man across from me says. He is gesturing toward the name tag I'm currently wearing.

"Thank you," I say, feeling the hoarseness in my throat. The waiting room is silent, and I can hear the big analog clock on the wall ticking quietly.

"Well, are you not going to ask my name?" the old man says light-heartedly, with a smile and a little laugh.

I smile sadly at him. This isn't a place where I feel the desire to smile or laugh. "What's your name?" I ask, merely to be polite, not caring about the answer.

"Arthur," he says simply, and holds out his hand. I lean forward pathetically and shake it. His hand is cold, yet soft.

"Nice to meet you, Julie," Arthur says, with the same sweet smile on his face.

I give him a half-smile as I lean back into my cold chair and shift my eyes to the tile floor. The cold, hard back of the seat hurts as my spine rubs against it. Each shift of my body only feeds my desire to get out of here, and Arthur is definitely not being helpful, trying to start a conversation with me when I'm feeling like this. I'm never in a mood to socialize when I'm trapped in this waiting room.

"Are you okay?" Arthur asks.

I look up, exhaustedly. I'm sure he means well, but I'd rather not talk with anyone right now.

"Fine," I say, "just tired of this waiting room."

"Ah," he says, "you must see it often."

I nod. "Seems like I'm here every week now. I'm sick of it."

Arthur nods, not sure of what to say. "Well," he pauses, "I'm sure it'll be okay – whatever it is that you're here for."

I sigh. "I don't know if it will, really." I pause, silently debating whether to go on or not. It's difficult trying to find the right words as I speak to Arthur.

"The doctor said it was only getting worse on the last visit," I continue, after a moment. "I just don't know what to do, really."

"They always seem to say that, don't they?" Arthur scoffs. "Almost seems like they want to worry us more."

"Seems that way sometimes."

"Must be why this waiting room is so nice: they worry us so much, and always make us come back to hear the same words, that the least they can do is make it a nice waiting room, right?"

I take a brief look around. The chairs are worn and seem long overdue for a visit to the dumpster. Dusty vases of fake azaleas sit on the few side tables which are placed at the ends of rows of chairs. The beige-tile floor is smudged from so many shoes scurrying on it.

The waiting room really isn't that nice, but I get the feeling Arthur is pathetically trying to find a positive in our situation of constantly having to see this room. Though I do admit the painted walls are rather nice; the peaceful blue color displayed around the room reminds me of the sky – which I'd much rather be looking at than the old, fluorescent lights buzzing in the ceiling.

"The paint on the walls is nice, I suppose," I respond.

"And the azaleas," Arthur says.

"Too dusty for my liking," I say, "and the outdated vases

don't seem to go with them."

"They're just a little old – like us," Arthur says. He's much more positive than I am.

"Well, I'm rather more fond of real flowers," I say, raining on Arthur's positivity.

"Oh, come on, now; they're doing the best they can. It wouldn't be too smart to have real flowers in a hospital, with their dirt and bugs, and whatever else flowers may track inside."

Well, I think to myself, still a little annoyed, *I can't argue with that*. "I guess so," I say, sensing the conversation coming to an end.

"I understand what you're saying, though," Arthur says, deciding to continue it, "real flowers are much more preferable – they're actually alive, after all."

I nod, giving him a small smile for trying so hard.

"But at least they chose a beautiful flower," Arthur continues. "For as long as I can remember, I've loved azaleas."

"I used to get azaleas quite often," I say, "but I don't

enjoy growing them as much as I used to."

"Why not?"

I sigh, feeling the tiredness in my body again. "They have a sort of bittersweetness to them, I suppose." I pause, failing in my attempt to find the right words to say to Arthur again. "It's not as enjoyable now that I don't have anyone to pick them off the bushes I used to grow, and put them in a vase for me."

"Ah," Arthur nods in understanding. "Did you and your husband used to do that?"

I nod quietly, biting at my thin, pale lips. I feel a twitch of pain invite itself inside me, though this time it isn't physical.

"Oh," Arthur says, with a hint of regret in his eyes, "I'm sorry, I shouldn't have asked."

I wave him off; "No, no, it's okay. I'm alright."

I admire Arthur's positivity, but the aspects of this waiting room that he sees as positive only seem negative in my eyes. The old-looking, fake azaleas, with the dusty vases that don't seem to go with them, only remind me that

I'm old, and that the moments which used to be perfect in my life have gone away now. They only remind me of when I used to receive those flowers, in mismatched yet thoughtful vases, to display throughout the house. I remember how I used to wish that my husband would have some sense of style when choosing the vases to put my azaleas in for me. How foolish I feel now, thinking about that; I'd give anything to see one of the ugly vases sitting here in the waiting room on the table when I returned home.

"Well," Arthur says, after a while, "I hope maybe someday you can enjoy growing your azaleas again." He pauses. "I'd love to pick them for you, if that would make you enjoy growing them again."

I feel a tear well up in my eye, but my shaky hand rubs it away before it can escape.

"Maybe I should just stop talking. I don't seem to be helping," Arthur says apologetically.

"No," I say, "it's just… that's kind of you. Thank you."

The desire to say more to him is strong, and screaming

inside me; I feel it pushing through, as if all the words in my body are about to spill out of my mouth. I sit in this crowded, uncomfortable waiting room, with a feeling I never thought I would have in a place like this.

Surprisingly, I feel this desire growing stronger in me more often than one would think: the desire to talk to someone who doesn't know me and tell them my life story – not because I feel they need to hear it, but because I feel I need to talk about it. I feel that if I talk about it enough, then maybe one day I'll be okay knowing that there are no more perfect moments for me.

How I miss the perfect moments I used to have. The sweet, perfect moments of my husband coming home with a new, ugly but thoughtful vase for the freshly-picked azaleas he'd gathered from the garden. Or the moments when we'd go outside and look at the beautiful view of the sky together. Many perfect moments, which seem to be trapped and distorted now, in this dreaded waiting room.

Now here I am, talking about these perfect past moments with someone who doesn't even know me, just to kill the tedious, tiresome waiting time.

It seems that time in this hospital waiting room grows longer with each visit, and the fake azaleas with the mismatched vases become dustier with every gaze.

Arthur

A Mini Date

"Oh," I say to Julie, "it wouldn't be a favor big enough to thank me for. I would love to have someone I could give flowers to."

She thanks me for offering to pick her flowers when she decides to grow her azaleas again – though it seems like more of a dream than a favor, picking flowers for a beautiful woman such as Julie, whom I've just met today in, of all places, the hospital waiting room.

She smiles sadly at me. She must be here for something quite worrisome, for she hasn't appeared happy throughout our whole time waiting together. She can't just be here for a simple checkup, like me.

I feel that I've been the cause of a sliver of her unhappiness right now, since I've unfortunately reminded her of a few events from her past which must upset her. But I can't stop myself from talking to her. She's sitting right across from me, with barely any leg room between us, and there's just something about her that feels sweet to me, something that draws me to her.

Whatever illness she must be here for has clearly given her great turmoil, and her mood seems to be one of great depth, from whatever it is she's endured. A part of me feels I should leave her alone, yet another part of me wants to talk to her for as long as we're in this waiting room together.

Yet another part of me wants to talk to her even longer, and take her on a date. I would call that the *stupid* part of me, since it's obvious she still misses her husband deeply. Maybe I shouldn't follow that foolish thinking and ask her on a date, but maybe I can do something else to bring out a little bit of positivity in her.

"It seems there are a lot of people ahead of us here," I say, as I look around at the crowded waiting room.

Julie nods. "Yeah, we'll probably be here a while." She sighs as if she hasn't slept last night.

"They may be fake azaleas here, but maybe there are

real ones outside, if you'd like to come with me to find out." I point to the direction sign hanging on the wall opposite us; among the chaos of titles and direction arrows is a row labeled *"Gardens"* with an arrow pointing to the right.

Julie turns around, seeming confused. "What are you pointing at?" she says, as she struggles to pull out a pair of reading glasses.

"There's a garden here. Seems like it'd be more enjoyable to look at than the dusty azaleas in here."

Julie turns back to me with a small smile on her face, which doesn't seem as sad as the ones before it. "Sure, that sounds nice," she says, and I feel my heart flutter.

We both stand, and I hear a tired groan from Julie as she does so. We make our way to one of the waiting room exits, with a few *excuse mes* along the way, and I push the door open for Julie. We stroll down a short hallway, until we're met by a glass door with a peaceful light shining through, clashing with the buzzing, fluorescent lights of the hospital.

We're hit by the warm outside as we walk out of the

cold, stuffy hospital hallway, into a small, yet beautiful garden filled with grass, flowers and a handful of trees. A few empty benches decorate the garden's shaded areas, and there is a small fountain in the center.

"Wow," Julie says as she looks around, now with a hint of interest in her eyes, "this is nice… for part of the hospital. Much better than inside."

I smile, happy to see her feeling something other than the sadness or exhaustion she's shown since I met her.

"Oh, look!" I say, as I notice the azalea shrub I'd hoped to see. I point it out to Julie, and we take a few steps through the fresh grass as we make our way toward it.

It's not the most beautiful of azalea shrubs, and many of its leaves are turning brown. It has obviously been here for quite some time, as it is taller than both of us. The branches, which were once covered in fluffy leaves and colorful flowers, have now been stripped to nothing but twigs and old stems. I find myself feeling a touch embarrassed for the poor shrub, as I glance at Julie looking at it. I feel that she must be disappointed, or even criticizing the shrub for its lack of flowers or bright, green leaves.

"Eh," I say, hesitantly, "I guess it might not be as great as I had hoped."

"It's still better than the fake ones inside," Julie says, lightly touching one of the branches. "These have grown; they haven't just sat there, forever stunted in growth and collecting dust, like the ones inside."

We're silent for a moment, as I let her admire the not-so-beautiful azalea shrub and listen to the faint sound of birds chirping in the trees.

"Although," Julie says, out of the silence, "I will say that its most perfect moments are probably over."

I turn to her. "Perfect moments?"

She looks to be lost in her thoughts, and turns to me with a hint of surprise in her eyes, as if caught saying something she shouldn't have.

"Uh," she stutters, "perfect blooms, I mean. It feels like there have been so many perfect blooms, with so many colorful azaleas, yet it seems so old now. That clearly doesn't happen anymore. It's so worn down, even the leaves on the branches seem to be struggling."

I shake my head; "Well, it might not have perfect blooms anymore, but I'm sure it has the odd, singular perfect bloom, every once in a while."

Julie smiles her sad smile again, and the feeling that she may be talking about more than just this old azalea shrub starts to grow inside me.

Then, a bright-pink color catches my eye. I look down and notice a small bunch of azaleas blooming, toward the bottom of the shrub.

"Hey," I say excitedly, "see? There's your perfect bloom." I point to them, and try to lift a few branches for Julie to see. She bends down slightly as she tries to catch a glimpse, and groans quietly.

"Oh!" she says, with a genuine smile, yet it seems almost as if tears are about to escape her soft, blue eyes at the same time.

"They might be a little harder to see now," I say, "but you only have to search a little."

"They're beautiful," Julie says in admiration.

After a moment of admiring the azaleas, we sit down on a wooden bench next to the shrub, under a shady tree. We don't talk much, yet it doesn't feel like a depressing or awkward silence, like it did in the waiting room; this feels more peaceful, as if each other's company is enough for us. We listen to the birds and Julie glances over at the azaleas every once in a while, while I glance over at her. Sometimes we share a comment about how beautiful the garden is, or Julie says how nice the sky looks today.

Now I know I'm crazy. I met this woman less than an hour or two ago, and I've heard from the shakiness in her voice just how deeply she must miss her husband whenever she mentions him, yet here I am already wanting to hold her hand, which sits resting next to mine on the bench.

I lightly place my hand on top of hers, then I quickly decide against it, pulling it back to my lap. "Sorry," I say, as I look away from her, feeling foolish.

Julie grabs my hand and places it back where it was. "It's perfectly okay," she says, with a little bit of color in her cheeks. We spend the rest of the time lightly holding hands, as we sit on the bench and continue admiring the garden in peaceful silence.

"I like this," Julie says simply after a moment, breaking the silence.

I smile. "I do, too."

She turns and looks me in my eyes, as if she's studying my face, searching for something that even I don't know is there.

"Do you ever feel like the perfect moments in your life are gone?" she asks suddenly.

I sigh at the sudden, heavy question, but I know my answer as soon as she asks it. "Of course not," I say. "Why, I feel perfect right now."

Julie laughs a little, and it makes me feel I'm in love.

"You think this is perfect?" she asks genuinely, with a small smile.

"I do. We even have azaleas here – not many, but still a perfect bloom, like you said earlier. This itself is a perfect moment."

Julie turns her head forward to face the garden. "Well,"

she pauses, “almost.”

Almost. That word seems to hang in the air.

What's not perfect about it?

I suddenly feel determined to give her the perfect moment she longs for. The perfect moment, I get the feeling, that she's missed for quite some time.

I've always been called a hopeless romantic, throughout my life, and I admit that I am. I fall in love easily and it's hard to pull myself out of it, even in old age. *Especially* in old age. And this woman, I get the feeling, is going to make me fall hard.

Who am I kidding? I've *already* fallen hard. I hate to admit it, with how little time we've spent together, but I know it. *Where has she been my whole life?* I wonder.

A side of me – the *very* foolish side of me, I know – wants to confess my love for her, right here and right now. I want to tell her about the connection I feel, how much I love her eyes and how happy it makes me to make her smile. We're old, so a part of me feels like no time should be wasted. That part of me wants me to propose right now and have the ceremony in this very garden. That part of me wants—

"Arthur?" Julie says, interrupting my daydreaming. I turn to her.

"Did you hear me? I think we should go inside. It's been a while, and we don't want to miss when we're called."

"Oh," I say disappointedly, secretly hoping for a confession of love from her instead. "Right, we probably should."

I stand up and offer my hand to help her up. Then we head back inside, to the gloomy, much less bright and much more dusty waiting room. As we walk through the doors, the waiting room is still crowded with people, but luckily we're able to regain our seats.

"I enjoyed that much more than having to sit in here," I say, as we plop down in the chairs.

Julie nods genuinely, speaking slowly and softly with what appear to be tears in her eyes, "I really did, too."

"Are you okay?" I ask. She's smiling, yet looks as if she's about to cry. I am intrigued to know why she's here.

What horrible pain or disease is making such a woman as this suffer? Whatever it is, I can only pray it's not fatal. I can only pray that she'll make it to the day when I can give her just one moment in her life which makes it feel perfect again.

Just one perfect moment.

Julie

Anxious

"I'm okay, Arthur," I say, as I hold back tears. I haven't been on a date in so long, and even though we merely walked a few steps, to a small garden connected to the hospital, I would still like to count that as a nice mini-date.

For a moment, I forgot the dreaded reason why I'm here. I forgot that my life felt as if it were falling apart, and that everything seemed to be going wrong. I forgot that I don't have anyone to pick me azaleas anymore. For a moment, I felt at peace. When Arthur took me to that garden, everything felt okay, even if the azalea shrub didn't have many blooms left; it was still beautiful and I still loved it – Arthur is the main reason for that. We didn't even really have many conversations or do too much on our mini-date, yet he so easily made me forget the world for a moment. It's obvious that's just who he is, and I long to go on more dates with him.

Now I'm back in this waiting room, where the only source of light for the dusty, fake azaleas is the annoyingly bright, fluorescent rectangles in the ceiling. The waiting room is still crowded, and it makes me uncomfortable, especially with how close I've gotten to crying in public.

I look over at Arthur, who's been staring at me the whole time since we got back from the garden.

"Maybe we should have stayed in the garden a little longer," he says, "the waiting room doesn't seem to help with calming your nerves."

"It certainly doesn't," I say, taking a deep, shaky breath.

"Would you like water from the vending machine? I noticed one just over there, around the corner." Arthur points in the direction we just came from.

I sigh: "Yes, that would be nice, actually."

"No problem. I'll be right back." Arthur stands and slowly makes his way through the waiting room, around the corner toward the vending machine.

What a sweet man. I can tell how hard he's tried to make this visit better for me, and I appreciate the effort and care.

It was clear that he wanted to stay longer in the garden, and I wanted to as well, but I can't miss this appointment – although it's probably going to go the same as it did the last time, and the same as before that. I'll be told it's getting worse, and I'll be offered another medication to try, or advised to keep trying the current medication, or doing this or that to slow the symptoms; to try this new method or that new exercise to help. I feel so sick of it all.

Yet here I am, in this stuffy waiting room, still anxious. Still anxious, nervous and, worst of all, hopeful that something different might happen this time; that maybe I'll get some small sliver of good news, instead of another false hope to cling to.

I could really use that water Arthur mentioned now. I turn around in my seat, to check if I can catch a glimpse of him, but I can't see around the corner from where I am. I turn back and glance at my watch; it's been a few minutes, and the vending machine is only a few feet away, right on the other side of the wall.

I make my way to my feet slowly, but still as quickly as I

can, and take a few steps to peek my head around the corner, feeling more than anxious now.

The vending machine area is empty; not a single person in sight.

Okay, no need to worry, I think to myself. *He's probably just in the restroom, or maybe he's just walked down the hall. Just try to relax.*

I walk to the vending machines, one selling drinks and another various snacks. "Arthur?" I say hesitantly to the air, but no response is given. The area is eerily quiet. I would enjoy the silence were I not so worried or alone.

I walk over to the restrooms, part of me feeling desperate enough to walk into the men's, to see if he's in there. A young man suddenly opens the door and exits the men's restroom.

"Oh, excuse me," I say, before he walks away, "did you happen to see an old man in there? Gray hair with glasses?"

The young man shakes his head. "No, ma'am, I was the only one in there. I did see someone heading that way when I walked in, though, if that helps." He points in the direction of the vending machines.

"Did he walk past the vending machines?" I ask, my worry growing with every moment that passes.

The young man nods, "I think so."

"Okay, thank you."

I turn and walk back in the direction I came from, passing the vending machines. The garden. It's in the direction I'm walking, in the same hallway. He must be there. At least, I hope he's there.

Please don't let me miss the appointment, I think to myself, as I wander swiftly down the hallway, away from the waiting room, to a man I've fallen in love with.

Arthur

Why Julie's Here

I sit on the bench in the garden, admiring the azalea shrub, along with the other flowers around me. It's such a beautiful day, and being out here is much better than being inside. The grass is green, the sky is clear and blue, like Julie's eyes, and the shade from the tree is the perfect touch. I feel like I could be out here for ages.

The glass door opens and Julie steps out, into the sun.

"Arthur! There you are!" she says, walking to me as fast as she can. She wraps her arms around me and hugs me tightly. "You had me worried for a moment."

I let out a small laugh and blush, as I feel her arms holding onto me. "Why? I'm just visiting the garden."

She sighs with relief as she lets go. "Come on," she says, "let's hurry back. We've been waiting long enough; I'm sure we won't be in that waiting room for too much longer."

I sigh disappointedly. What if we go back and her name is called first, and then she hurries off? What if I don't get her phone number or her email before then? What if we go back into that waiting room, and after that I never see her again?

I can't let that happen.

"Will we see each other again after our appointments?" I ask, refusing to move from the bench until I get an answer.

Julie sighs, "Yes, we will."

"Do you want to?"

"Of course I want to. You're sweet, Arthur."

I feel butterflies in my stomach. That's a good enough promise for me. I stand up and follow her back to the waiting room.

As we sit back down, I can tell that Julie is a little flustered. She takes a deep breath and sits up, not leaning back in the chair.

"Julie, are you okay?" She's probably tired of me asking that.

She sighs, "Yes, Arthur, I'm okay."

We sit for a few more minutes, neither of us talking.

"Martin," a doctor's voice calls out, as she stands in the open doorway with a clipboard, facing the waiting room.

Julie stands, gathering her purse together, and my heart pounds, knowing that she's about to leave.

The doctor spots Julie. "Julie Martin? Nice to see you. Where's Arthur?"

"He's right here," Julie says, gesturing to me. I turn to the doctor in confusion, as Julie looks at me with her comforting, blue eyes.

"Honey," she says, grabbing my hand gently, "the doctor called us. Let's go."

Julie

My Husband

That was so foolish of me, just letting him go off on his own like that, to get me a drink from the vending machine, knowing full well his condition. I just got caught up in the moment, thinking how sweet he was being to me, without even knowing who I am. How caring it was to take me to the garden, to see the azaleas. I forgot for a moment that he has dementia. But the vending machine was only right around the corner; I thought it would be okay, that he wouldn't forget what he was doing and wander off, like he does so often now. I should have known better than that.

Arthur sits on the leather couch next to me, as we wait for the doctor to come back into the room. His eyes stay fixed on the floor, a look of pain on his face. We're quiet after the doctor leaves to take care of something, and I gently hold his hand as we sit in silence.

"I love you," Arthur says, still keeping his gaze on the

floor. I look over to him and squeeze his hand comfortingly.

He looks up, into my eyes. "Are you my wife?"

"Yes, honey," I say simply, having been asked this question multiple times since he was put in the retirement home, away from me.

Our daughter picks him up and drives him here to drop him off, since she lives closer to the retirement home. She always leads him right to his seat, telling him to sit and not move unless the name "Martin" is called. If the waiting room is crowded, she tells him, "Save the seat next to you for Julie. She'll be here soon, to wait with you." Sometimes he remembers to save the seat for me, sometimes he forgets and sometimes, like today, he remembers to save the seat but not who for.

My eyes light up when I walk through the waiting-room doors and see him. I've hated living alone in our big, empty house without him. I absolutely hated it when he had to be separated from me, so that he could be taken care of somewhere else, twenty-four-seven. I check the sign-in desk to make sure our daughter has signed him in, then approach the empty seat next to Arthur.

"Oh, this seat's taken," he says, and my excitement fades. I am reminded of why we're here in this stuffy, depressing waiting room. I am reminded of how tired I am, both physically and emotionally.

I've argued with him in the past, but today I just couldn't seem to find the energy to do it, so I sat in the seat across from him, instead. I've never done that before today, and a part of me is actually rather happy that I did. A part of me is happy not to argue with him today, and see the hurtful confusion on his face when I try to explain who I am to him, because then we would have just sat in silence as we waited. Or he would have continued arguing that I shouldn't be sitting in the seat he'd saved for someone else.

Today, I got to see him fall in love with me again. It's something quite bittersweet to think about. It makes me smile, while also bringing tears to my eyes. He's forgotten who I am, yet I know he still loves me.

"Am I going to forget you again?" he asks, his eyes desperate and concerned.

I'm quiet for a moment, and I shift my eyes down and away from his.

"It... it doesn't matter..." I say, "I'll still love you, either way, Arthur."

"But you don't deserve to be forgotten."

My eyes start to water. It feels as if I cry at every visit here. "You don't know who I am; how do you know I don't deserve it?" I say, bitterly.

"Maybe I don't remember some things," he says, "but that doesn't mean I don't *know* some things, and I know that you don't deserve it."

I laugh quietly. "That doesn't make any sense," I say.

"Sure it does," he says. "I don't remember you, but I *know* I love you."

I look up at him again, his eyes still locked on me.

"And what if you forget that you love me one day?"

"Then I'll just fall in love with you again." He squeezes my hand gently. "Maybe next time we can go on a date to the vending machine, and you can tell me your favorite snack, instead of flowers."

I laugh, yet a few tears escape my eyes at the same time. I wrap my arms around Arthur and hug him tight, holding him as if the tighter I do so, the longer I might get to keep my husband here with me before he forgets me again.

Arthur

Her Perfect Moment

The appointment is confusing. A doctor comes in, acting as if she has known me for quite some time. I am asked countless questions, and I can't find the answers to most.

Now I am given sympathetic smiles from other doctors and therapists, as Julie and I walk down the hallway to exit.

It's quite a terrifying and unsettling feeling, having everyone know you and things about you, when you'd swear you've never met any of them in your entire life. It makes the entire hospital feel wrong, almost as if it were a dream.

Is this how I feel every time I come here? I think to myself, though not being able to answer the question.

"I love you," I say to Julie again, as we exit the hallway and make it back to the stuffy waiting room, where it all started (well, at least where I *thought* it all started).

When we were sitting on the couch, waiting for the

doctor together, I wanted to confess my love for her. *What better moment to confess your love than the moment when you're reminded that she's your wife?* I'd thought to myself.

"I love you, too," Julie says.

We make our way to the front exit doors, and I suddenly feel a rush of panic. I pause and stop my legs from moving.

Julie sighs, as if I do this every time. "Honey," she says sympathetically, and tired, "I hate it, too, okay? But we have to go. How about we go eat somewhere together, before you go back?"

I look around the room, searching desperately for a distraction from leaving. I notice the blue paint on the walls, the cheap chairs lined up in rows, the vases that sit on the few tables in the room, with their fake azaleas.

The azaleas.

I don't waste a moment hesitating. I turn around and start walking in the opposite direction, knowing exactly where I'm going.

"Arthur," Julie says behind me, a lot slower than me; it's

hard for her to keep up. "Arthur, where are you going? Come on."

I turn the corner, and don't stop until I make it to the glass door with sunlight shining through. I open the door and step outside, into the fluffy grass, and walk straight to the azalea shrub. Julie follows behind me and makes it outside, breathing a little bit heavier than usual.

"Arthur, honey, what are you doing? We have to go," she says.

I look at the azalea shrub. There are a few blooms on it. Pink azaleas decorate the worn-down shrub, and I pick off a few twigs with the most perfect blooms I can find.

I turn around and face Julie. "This," I say simply, "is what you needed for your perfect moment." I hand her the azaleas.

She's stunned for a moment. Stunned that I found a way to remember what she wanted. She's quiet as her shaky hand grabs the azaleas.

"If I'm going to forget you," I say, "I want you to at least try not to forget me. When you need more to admire, and to remember that I love you, you only have to remind me, and I'll pick more for you to put in the house. Maybe I'll even get a vase somehow, too."

Julie

My Perfect Moment

He did it. He really did it. He remembered what I wanted.

I thought my perfect moments were over. I thought they had been long gone, when I realized his dementia had made him start forgetting me; when he was put in the retirement home; when I realized that I am going to be in our house alone now. Yet, here he is. I'm holding flowers right now that he just picked for me. Flowers that *he,* my husband, has picked for me. I blush. I cry. I smile. I feel butterflies in my stomach. I feel everything hit me all at once.

My husband is standing in front of me, smiling, having just handed me the azaleas I've missed for so long now. I kiss him. I kiss the man I love. The man who I feel I haven't had in centuries. The man who forgets everything, but has such a deep love for me that he hasn't forgotten that. Maybe he forgot who I was, but he didn't forget that he loves me.

"Thank you," I say. It's a simple response, but the emotion I feel behind it is strong and deep.

A perfect moment. My husband has given me another perfect moment, after so long.

"Are you happy?" Arthur asks, with hope in his eyes.

I nod and hug him. "Yes, I'm happy. This is perfect, Arthur."

This moment may not look perfect to others. We're an old couple, neither of us considered young and attractive anymore. One of us has dementia and one is in what seems like constant pain now, from the struggles of getting old. We're in a hospital garden which is small with old, wilting plants. It surely doesn't look perfect, but it is for us.

I have my husband in front of me, who has just picked me flowers – my favorite flowers, in fact. I have my husband, who I love dearly and who loves me, even when he forgets me.

I have Arthur, who, after all these years, is still able to give me those perfect moments in life that everyone needs.

Perfect moments can be more common than one may notice, even if they're small and simple. In fact, the small and simple are usually the greatest.

A Pale Amaryllis

Annika Galloway

Amaryllis,
symbolizing strength, beauty and
determination.

Trapped

The chair broke. My god, the chair actually broke! All I did was sit down, just like everyone else, but no one else's chair broke.

"Sweetie, it's okay. I promise, it's not your fault," the receptionist says, as I awkwardly stand in the hospital waiting room while she pulls the chair out of the row, away from all the others.

I feel like I could cry right about now. I feel so embarrassed, I wish I could just disappear. People in the waiting room are staring now.

They always stare.

The receptionist takes one look at my body and embarrassed facial expression, and knows exactly what I'm thinking. "Oh, sweetie," she says, sympathetically, "I swear it's not because of your weight. These chairs are old and outdated, and this one was just ready to break. Okay?"

I nod quietly as she takes the chair away. Mom sits down

in one of the old hospital chairs while I continue standing.

"Diana," Mom says to me, "are you going to sit or just stand there the whole time?"

"I'm fine standing," I say, afraid to sit down and break another chair.

"There are a lot of people here today. We're probably going to be waiting a while, you know."

I nod, already feeling tired. "I know."

"Diana, look at you. You're not going to be able to stand for long; you'll get tired. Now, just sit down."

I sigh. I press down on the chair next to Mom's with my hand.

"You're not going to break it. Just sit," Mom says, annoyed.

I sit in the chair nervously, afraid to put all of my weight on it. The chair doesn't break. Thank goodness.

"Stop worrying so much," Mom says. "We're here to get you help."

"Mom, just stop," I say.

"What? All I said was—"

"Mom, can we just stop talking about my weight, please?" My cheeks turn red and I feel the embarrassment grow.

"Okay, okay, whatever," she responds.

Thank you. Finally! I think to myself. We're silent – just how things should be – as we wait for our name to be called.

I look around the waiting room, praying I don't catch anyone staring at me. The room is lined with old and outdated chairs, though I know being cheap and old isn't the reason my chair broke and no one else's did. There are side tables at the ends of the rows of chairs, with fake amaryllis flowers in mismatching vases, to pathetically decorate the room. They make me think of the amaryllises Dad used to give Mom to decorate the table, while we ate dinner together.

The walls are painted a calm blue color – almost the same color as the ocean, that time when I went to the beach with my friend Alise and my family. It was so clear and crystal blue that day. That was the time when I used to be comfortable wearing a bikini. If I wore one now, I'm afraid people would just stare, especially at my stomach. I look down at all the ugly fat on my body and put my hand over my midriff, as if that will cover up all that's there.

"Diana," Mom says. I look up and she's giving me that same look she always gives me.

"What," I say, annoyed.

"Stop."

"Stop what?"

"You know what. You're getting inside your head again. No one is staring at you and you're not ugly."

I scoff. Easy for her to say; she doesn't look like me.

"What did you eat for breakfast this morning?" Mom asks. I hate it when she asks me anything about food; I'm obsessed with it enough already.

I look down. "Nothing. Just water," I say.

"You do that every time: whenever you know you're about to get weighed, or you know we're going somewhere like this, you never eat that morning, as if that's going to help you."

I rest my elbow on the arm of the chair and plop my chin into my hand, sighing. I wish Mom would just shut up already.

"You're only fifteen years old," Mom begins. "I just don't understand how such a young, beautiful girl could end up like this."

"*Mom*, just stop! Please!" She always does this.

"Diana, I'm just worried for you."

"Yeah, I got that."

"I just want you to be healthy."

"Well, you said that's why we're here, so why do you keep bringing that up, like I don't already know it?"

Mom sighs and stops talking.

We used to not be like this. We used to be close, but things started changing the moment I let the monster in my head take over my body. The monster that makes me absolutely obsess over food. The monster that makes me lie awake some nights thinking about food, thinking about when and what I'll eat next. And, when I do eat, thinking about what a poor decision I'm making, as I stuff the unhealthy food choice in my mouth.

Mom is just worried. I know that, but I wish she knew how to worry better.

We used to eat together. We'd cook together, sit down with the rest and eat at the dinner table, like a normal, healthy family. Dad would give Mom her bright-red amaryllises, to put in the glass vase sitting in the middle of the table, for everyone to admire while we ate, talked and laughed together. We don't do much of that anymore – not after they started noticing changes in my weight.

I couldn't handle the little things. I couldn't handle the little comments with the slight tone of concern, which I'd start receiving from Mom. I couldn't handle the little gestures and glances I'd get from everyone, especially my siblings. Even the amaryllises, in their beautiful glass vase, seemed to be changing, as if they were mocking me. They started to lose their vibrant, radiant color, which used to carry beauty to everyone's eyes. Their red, which used to be the first thing anyone noticed when walking into the room, was growing paler and weaker with each new bouquet of flowers Dad would bring home. All of these little things only seemed to get worse over time, and would cause another long night of dreadful fixation on every little detail at the table.

I remember when my plate started looking different from that of my parents and siblings; how, when Mom was making a plate for me, she would put a few extra servings on it. Rhea, my older sister, would sit next to me with a plate that was smaller than mine. Donovan, my younger brother, would often be caught staring at me as I ate, as if it were such a fascinating sight to see his fat sister make a fool of herself as she stuffed food in her face. I must have eaten the whole plate, with extra servings, only a few times before I noticed how different it was from that of the rest of my family.

"Diana," Mom would say, "do you want any more?" She would ask it so sweetly, I remember. I would look down at my plate, with only a few bites taken from it, and shake my head no, knowing full well that I did, in fact, want a lot more.

"Come on," she would say, "I gave you a little extra. You're usually hungrier than Rhea and Donovan."

"No, I don't need any more," I would say. Then I'd walk back to my room and think of every moment Donovan stared at me, and every instance when Mom or Dad would glance up at me, probably wondering if they should add more to my plate. It was almost like a game of torment I'd play with myself: *How many times Donovan stared at you equals two points of insecurity! Every time Mom asks if you're going to eat more food is another point of anxiety!* I started winning this game every night, after dinner.

Now I eat alone, too ashamed to eat in front of anyone else.

"Do you want anything?" Mom's voice snaps my mind back to the waiting room.

"Huh?" I say.

Mom points toward the vending machine right outside the waiting room. "They might have a few healthy snacks you'd like to eat."

I roll my eyes. *Really?* I think to myself. *You're really trying to make me eat right now?* "No," I say simply, feeling uncomfortable at even the slight mention of food.

Mom sighs and leaves her chair, to make her way toward the vending machine.

I sit in silence again in the crowded waiting room, watching the occasional person filter in and out, and eyeing the dust collected on the fake amaryllises. This is the second time I've visited this place, and the process is still new to me.

I grow more anxious with each passing minute, afraid of hearing my name being called. My hands feel clammy and my legs are restless. I grab a strand of my hair and loop it around my finger – something I usually do when I'm feeling uncomfortable, or don't know what to do with my hands. My brown hair is so thin and feels oily today.

Of course, I think to myself. *Of all the days, today my hair just isn't working with me.*

I stand up, too restless and nervous to continue sitting. I wander around the area for a moment, until I find a restroom, passing Mom at the vending machine. I catch a glimpse of the mini cinnamon rolls sitting right in the middle of the machine as I pass; my stomach growls and a wave of guilt instantly smacks me.

I open the door to the restroom and thank God it's empty. I walk to the sink farthest from the door and lean my arms against the counter, already feeling tired from walking here. I look up into the mirror and, sure enough, my hair is a mess.

I'm a mess.

To add to the mess, my white skin is hideously pale, except for my red cheeks – probably from all the embarrassment and shame I've felt today. I put my hand up to my cheek, feeling the chubbiness under my pale skin.

I take a deep, shaky breath.

I pull the hair tie off my wrist, and put my hair into a ponytail as best as I can, pathetically trying to smooth it out and pat down any puffs which stick out.

I look pathetic.

The water from the sink is cold as I turn it on, and I wish I could splash it in my face, but I put on makeup today, hoping that people might stare at that rather than my body – as if that *ever* works. I grab a paper towel and wet it slightly, then wipe it around my face pitifully, trying not to mess up any of my makeup.

I look the same.

For a moment, I just stare at the hideous reflection in the mirror.

How did I even manage to get like this? I think to myself.

I think back to the mini cinnamon rolls I saw a moment ago, before coming in here. My hand involuntarily goes to my stomach, feeling the fat that surrounds me.

Not me; the fat traps *me* in this dreaded body.

I can't go into the doctor's office looking like this! my mind tells me.

The image of the doctor from my last visit pops into my head. Dr. Anderson. He looks so young, and it's obvious that he goes to the gym. His thick, brown hair is just the perfect length to run hands through, his eyes a sharp, piercing green, and his smile totally lit up the entire room.

And his freckles! Oh, his freckles are what really make my stomach turn. Everything about him just looks so perfect and beautiful.

Aaaannnndddd then there's me, I think, as I stare at myself in this mirror. I look *so* pathetic. I turn sideways and suck in my stomach, to see if that makes the fat go away. It doesn't.

I sigh. There's no way I can make myself look how I want to within an hour, or however long I'll be waiting for my name to be called. Dr. Anderson could be out there right now, waiting on me, for all I know.

The door to the restroom opens and I jump. A lady casually walks in and enters a stall, though not without glancing at me first, then immediately turning away from me. My nose feels a slight sting as I feel my eyes getting ready to weep. I wipe them before any tears can fall and leave the restroom, shyly and awkwardly making it back to my chair, next to Mom in the waiting room. I hate saying "excuse me" to people, as my body slides its way through the crowdedness. It makes me wish I could just disappear.

"You okay?" Mom asks, as I sit back in my chair cautiously, afraid it might break again. She's eating a bag of chips she got from the vending machine.

"Fine," I say, as I watch her toss a chip into her mouth.

"Are you *sure* you don't want anything from the vending machine?" Mom insists. "You're watching my bag of chips like a hawk."

I shake my head, half to say no and half to snap myself out of staring.

"Diana," she says, turning her Mom voice on, "there's no harm in just getting a snack." She hands me two dollars. "Go get a bag of peanuts or… just, *something*. I've heard your stomach growling quite a bit now."

I throw the money back at her. "Mom, just stop! I don't want anything." She makes this so much harder.

Mom sighs and reluctantly puts the money back into her wallet. "Please, just let me know if you change your mind. We might be here a while; you can see how crowded this place is today."

I know I won't change my mind. Not with how my body

is now, and not with having to see Dr. Anderson in a little while.

Mom rests her elbow on the armchair and puts her face in her hand. She looks stressed. Her eyes drift toward me and look down at me. I know what she's thinking, but I don't say anything – I mean, what *can* I say in a situation like this? A situation where my eating habits are so bad that I could die if I don't get help?

"I pray this appointment helps. You can't possibly live like this…" Mom whispers.

I hate the little comments she makes when she's thinking out loud.

Although, she's right: I haven't lived in a long time.

Memories

The worst part was when people at school started noticing.

"You grow when you hit middle school," my parents would tell me. "Of course a few clothes might feel a bit tight; it's completely normal."

I know this is true, but it felt different for me, like growing wasn't the only reason my clothes weren't fitting anymore.

I guess it looked different to my classmates, too, based on the comments I started getting, and the whispers I'd hear as I walked down the hallways. No one else seemed to get the kind of comments I'd get just because they were "growing." Of course, the cafeteria and the gym were the two worst places on Earth for me to be during those times. The cafeteria never had good food anyway, but it tasted amazing (not just for me, but everyone) after five periods when eating in the classrooms wasn't allowed. I'd always get the cookies they served for dessert, along with two of whatever entrée they'd be serving that day.

"Diana," a perky voice said once. It was one of the popular girls (something every girl wanted to be in middle school); she was standing over me, with her friends by her side, as I was about to take a bite into my taco. I looked up to see her analyzing every piece of food on my plate. Her eyes drifted over the two cookies, two tacos and the extra scoop of corn I'd pleaded the lunch server for, plus my soda.

She leaned on the table and tilted her head. "What are you bulking up for?" she asked.

I suddenly felt fatter.

"Mind your business," I said, setting down my taco.

The girl (part of her was probably pissed that I didn't take the time to learn her name, like everyone else in the school) had a fake expression of shock on her face. "What? I'm just curious what sport you're in!" She knew as well as I did that I wasn't in any kind of sport. I couldn't pass one of those required physicals to start a sport, anyway, even if

I wanted to.

"I'd *love* to help out," she continued. "I could get you another taco, to help you fatten up faster— I mean *bulk* up faster."

"Are you really that bored with your life that you have to try to ruin someone else's to make yourself feel better?" I said, throwing up a pathetic wall to appear strong and not actually hurt.

"Whatever. Was just trying to help," she said, as she walked away with her friends – all probably as fake as her.

I wanted to get up and throw my food in the trash, then walk right out of the school and never come back. I wanted to disappear. I always want to disappear.

I can't, though. I couldn't even throw away my food until the popular girl was out of sight, because I couldn't show any sign of hurt or weakness. Those aren't things you can show in middle school.

I'd tried to stop eating at the dinner table at home, and now here. Where was I supposed to eat now, if I couldn't feel safe from judgment eating at home or school?

I stopped getting extra food in the cafeteria during lunch, even if eating didn't seem to fill my stomach like it did everyone else's. Everyone else was probably eating at home, too, but even then I felt people were staring and judging.

Except for one day, one lunch period, for one single moment. There was one single moment when I felt like I didn't want to disappear, for once.

"Hey," a boy said, as he took a seat across from me – something which wasn't allowed then; everyone had to sit at the assigned table, with whatever class they were in at the time.

I looked up from my tray in confusion. "Hey," I said back. He was kind of cute.

He looked down, sort of shyly. "So, I was just kind of wondering…"

There were no thoughts in my mind, just the nervous and excited feeling of what this boy would say next.

"Would you wanna go out with me?"

I felt butterflies do flips inside my stomach. Did he

really just say what I thought he said? And so up-front, too? This was a big deal. It was what every middle schooler dreamed of here. He was cute, too! I couldn't believe this was happening.

"Oh—" I responded with surprise, but was immediately cut off.

"Just kidding!"

He ran back to the table he came from, and sat down with a group of other boys, who were laughing.

"I'm choosing 'truth' next time," he said. He then pointed to the boy across from him, "Alright, your turn: truth or dare?"

And, back to wanting to disappear…

What was I thinking? Of course a boy wasn't going to want to be with someone like me. My body was just too fat. I could feel it.

I started trying my best to eat wherever people were not, then started trying to eat in secret, as if that would make me appear less fat.

High school seems to be a little better than middle

school. There are no assigned tables in the cafeteria, so I can sit alone or with a few acquaintances if I want. But what I prefer most of the time, and usually choose to do, is eat in the classroom. The teacher doesn't mind, and it's a quiet space where I know no one will hurt me, because there is no one around to do that.

Oh, but I can't wait until I get a car! When I get a car and can drive myself to school, I won't have to worry about lots of things. During lunch, I can sit in my car and eat, and not have to worry about any eyes staring at me, or any whispers, as I take a bite into some unhealthy food choice or other. I won't have to worry about riding the dreaded bus to and from school anymore. I'll be free from all of that, and it will be amazing.

"Can I drive home after this?" I ask Mom, as we continue to wait in the waiting room. I want to make sure I practice enough that I can get my license as soon as I turn sixteen. I don't want any time wasted.

"Well…" Mom says, hesitantly, "I don't know. Maybe."

I look at her in confusion. "What do you mean, maybe?

You always let me drive, unless the road has too many complicated turns or something. It didn't seem too bad on the way here; we didn't make many left turns."

"No, you're right, it's just that I wanted us to go somewhere other than home after."

"Where are we going, then? Maybe I could drive there."

Mom sighs. "Remember China Cafa? The restaurant that misspelled 'café' and was owned by that sweet Chinese couple? We haven't been there in a while, and I remember how much you used to love going there. I thought maybe we could stop by there after."

Aggravation fills my mind and I sigh, heavily. "Mom, come on!" I say, annoyed. Why does she always have to do this? She always offers me food, as if she doesn't know I'm already tempted enough.

"What?" She says, "I miss their egg rolls. Don't you?"

"Ughh!" I put my face in my hands.

"Okay, okay. Let's just see how you feel after this appointment; if you're feeling hungry by then or not. Okay?"

"Fine," I say. But being hungry isn't the issue; I'm already hungry. I'm *always* hungry. I already know I'll want food after this appointment, but I don't want to look like this anymore. I don't want to feel trapped in this fat anymore, so I can't keep eating everything Mom tempts me to eat.

"Do you remember the last time we went?" Mom asks me, nostalgically. "It was so long ago, wasn't it?"

I nod.

"It's kind of my go-to memory, whenever I need to think of a simple time," she continues. "It was long before this whole problem started. Donovan and Rhea were at a friend's house, and your dad and I played outside with you, not a care in the world. Then, when we all got hungry, none of us overthought it; we all just got in the car and drove around, looking for a new place to eat. Then we found that weird Chinese place with the misspelled 'café', and decided to try it. It ended up being amazing, and it put us all in an even better mood. Do you remember that day?"

I nod. "Yeah, it was good."

That was a good day. It was a time before I had to always worry about food and what I ate, then feel guilty whenever I made the wrong food choice. It was a time when I could just enjoy myself.

"Do you have a memory like that? One you always go to, of a simpler time?"

"I don't know," I say. I notice the calm blue paint on the walls again and think of the beach trip. "The time we went to the beach and you let me bring Alise, I guess."

"Oh, yeah, that was a nice time," Mom says. "I haven't seen Alise in a while. Do you still talk much with her? We could invite her on our next beach trip."

"Yeah, we still talk pretty often." Though that is true, I don't know how I feel about inviting her on our next beach trip. I don't even know how I feel about a next beach trip at all. Yes, the last beach trip was a good memory, and a lot was simple then, but that's not how things are anymore, and going back to a place that has simple memories isn't going to guarantee that it'll be simple again. In fact, going back to a place with simple memories, while things are complicated, will probably only tarnish the simple memories you had before.

"Do you see her often anymore?" Mom asks.

I shake my head. "Not as often as I used to. We just kind of text now."

Mom nods in understanding, not sure what to say.

Alise and I used to hang out often, but after my body got to how it is now, I tend to not really go out with anyone at all anymore. It's just easier that way. I get tired too easily and I can't handle it when people stare, so it's better and more comfortable for me to just stay in.

I remember the last time Alise and I went out, like we used to do so often. We were at a mall, walking around like usual…

"Are you okay?" Alise had asked, when she started noticing me getting a little slower in our walking. She didn't look concerned, like most people do. She was always good at hiding that under the chilled expression she'd hold for me, knowing a concerned look wasn't going to make me feel any more confident.

"Yeah, just tired today, I think," I said. I was much more than just tired, but I felt too embarrassed to tell Alise that I needed to sit down.

"Let's get some smoothies and sit down somewhere. I'm kind of tired of walking, too."

She was so sweet. It was obvious my body wasn't looking how it used to, but Alise didn't have to make a scene out of that fact. She knew how to make me feel less embarrassed in situations like this. She never asked if I needed to sit down, which would have made me feel awkward, but she would offer a situation where she could sit down with me and not make a big deal out of it.

"Oh, yeah, I'd love a smoothie right now," I said, appreciating the offer.

We walked a little further toward the smoothie shop and I could already see little black spots forming in my eyes. All of my energy was escaping me, but I could see the smoothie shop just a few shops down, so I pushed myself, too embarrassed to ask Alise to slow down even more.

Other people were out there right then, exercising, by

running in their neighborhoods, parks, on treadmills and more. I felt like one of these people with every outing. I felt out of breath. I felt my energy leaving me, and like I was going to pass out. What more do you need for it to qualify as a hardcore run?

"Diana?" I heard Alise's voice say. She looked concerned now, her chilled expression gone, which was rare for her. She leaned in closer to me, her eyebrows furrowed in worry, and… why was the ceiling behind her now? Wait, how was she kneeling down, looking at me?

Alise put her hand on my shoulder and nudged me carefully. "Diana? Are you okay? Can you stand?"

I turned my head and winced. A bulging pain throbbed at the back of my head, and my hand immediately pressed against it. I was at eye level with a bunch of shoes, some standing still and some scurrying about.

Alise winced watching me wince. "Ooh, it had to be a tile floor!" She looked up and around at her surroundings, with wide-eyed panic filling her face. "God, I don't know what to do! I'm calling your mom, okay, Diana? Don't worry, you'll be fine, you'll be fine."

I felt multiple voices coming in, close around Alise and I.

"Is she okay?"

"Does she need paramedics?"

"Do you need anyone to call 911?"

"Where are y'all's parents?"

My eyes widened as I gained a sense of my surroundings, and I sat up quickly, instantly regretting doing it so fast. My head was swimming in a throbbing pain. I grabbed it and held it tight, as if it were about to fall off.

"I'm fine, I'm fine," I said to the air, not sure exactly who I was talking to, only knowing that I wanted everyone to go away and stop staring at me. I knew everyone was looking at me and, after taking one look at my body, I knew exactly what everyone was thinking.

"Yeah, she just passed out," I could hear Alise say, with the phone up to her ear. "Yeah, she's awake – she's sitting up, but she hit her head on tiles, so—"

I looked up and saw a few strangers standing over me, along with Alise, who was kneeling down. *I would love to disappear right now,* I thought. They all had that look – that dreaded look I always get: a poorly hidden reaction to how my body looks.

"Diana," Alise said, "can you talk to your mom?" She held out her phone, and I hesitantly pulled a hand away from my head to grab it. I held the phone up to my ear.

"Hello?"

"Diana!" Mom said, frantically, "Are you okay? I'm on my way to pick you girls up. Do you need to go to the hospital? What happened? Is your head bleeding? Tell all those people to give you some space; they don't need to be crowding you right now."

"Mom, I'm fine, I'm fine, I'm fine! Just come pick us up. I want to go home."

A stranger handed me an unopened bottle of water he'd just got from the vending machine, and I accepted it gratefully – while also feeling like I wished he'd go away, along with everyone else.

"Let's try to stand, and walk over to sit on that bench right there, okay?" Alise said, as she tugged at my arm gently. I was more than willing to cooperate; I needed to get out of this embarrassingly bright spotlight. I stood up slowly, with Alise's help, and took a few steps to the bench, with fake plants on either side. I plopped down in the seat next to Alise and took a deep breath.

"Is your mother coming, sweetie?" a lady asked, as the gathered people started to go about their day again.

"She's coming," Alise answered for me. "We're just going to wait here until she gets here. We're all good now, thank you."

The lady nodded worriedly, but continued along her way, like everyone else, after briefly looking me up and down, with a concerned look in her eyes.

Now it was just me and Alise, though I still felt like everyone was too close – or, more accurately, everybody's eyes were.

Alise and I were silent and it was painfully awkward, though I felt like talking would be worse. We both cared for each other deeply, and we'd both been well aware that there was a problem, but never quite talked about it. We'd never gotten into the deep conversation of feelings or concerns – I guess now we were at the point where we were forced to have those conversations. At least, that's how Alise must have felt.

"I'm sorry that happened, Diana," Alise said.

What could I say to something like that? *"It's okay?"* No, because it wasn't okay. I settled for, "It's not your fault."

Silence again.

"I know we don't really say it often," Alise said, "but you know I'm here for you, right?"

I nodded awkwardly. "Yeah, I know."

There was a pause, and I knew Alise wanted to say something else, but her hesitation filled the air around us.

"You seem like you want to say something else," I said.

"It's just…" more hesitation, "I don't want you to feel judged, but I'm worried. I'm worried about you and… Don't you think your weight is starting to get a little out of hand?"

A heaviness swam in the air, and I felt my cheeks get hot with embarrassment from the word "weight." I didn't say anything. I didn't know what to say.

"I just say this because I care about you," Alise continued. "I mean, it's like you have no energy anymore. It's hard to even go on a walk through the mall now."

"I was just tired today," I said, simply.

"Diana, you passed out and hit your head. I'd say that's a little more than just being *tired*."

"But I'm fine," I lied, as my head bulged with pain.

"I'm sorry but, no, you're not. This is getting dangerous, Diana."

I felt that was a little dramatic. Dangerous? *Come on, Alise!*

"Listen," Alise said, "I just want you to know I'm here for you. I don't want you to feel judged or like you're not cared for. I'll help you through this – if you'll let me."

Alise's phone buzzed, and she pulled it out of her pocket to answer it.

"Hey," Alise said into the phone. "Okay, let me ask her."

She turned to me. "Your mom's here. Are you ready to walk to the parking lot, or do you want her to come in here first?"

I thought about Mom coming in here, with her frantic manner, and instantly knew my answer. "Let's walk to the parking lot. Tell her to just wait in the car."

Alise nodded and repeated what I'd said into the phone. "Alright, we'll be there in a minute," she said, then put her phone back into her pocket.

"Ready?" she asked.

I nodded, taking a deep breath, afraid of what could go wrong on the journey back to the parking lot. I wasn't ready to face embarrassment again, but that was a risk I had to take if I wanted to get out of here.

The Scale

I haven't seen Alise since that day at the mall. We still text quite often, but Alise has learned now to give up asking me if I want to meet up or go out.

I just *hate* when people stare.

I can't handle it – and I won't if I can help it.

Here in this waiting room, though, I'm forced to handle it.

That day at the mall is the reason I'm here now. I guess passing out from a simple mall walk was the final straw for Alise and my family. They all agreed without me that it's time for me to get help. They all agreed that it's time to start going to these dreaded appointments.

My phone buzzes in my pocket, and a few people in the waiting room glance up at me. I shift uncomfortably in my chair as I pull my phone out of my pocket. Alise's name pops up on the lock-screen, with her contact picture from simpler times. It was taken on the day we went to an ice cream shop, after she'd gotten blue box braids in her thick, dark hair and it looked amazing. Her dark-brown skin made the royal blue color pop, and the pink strawberry ice cream she held only added to the perfect picture.

"How'd your 2nd appointment go?" the text reads.

"Still in the waiting room," I text back.

"Wow, you've been there a while," she responds.

"Yeah. Sucks."

My stomach growls and I throw my hand onto my stomach, like I always do, hoping to somehow hide what everyone just heard.

"It's okay, I'm hungry, too," Mom says. "Those chips did not do the trick."

Embarrassment fills my head. Again. Oh, how I wish I could just disappear. How I *always* wish I could disappear.

I want to get this whole day over with, so I can go home and lock myself in my room, where no one can see me and the only person left to judge my appearance is myself.

"Diana Walker."

I snap out of my head and look up to see Dr. Anderson

holding a clipboard, standing in the doorway to the waiting room. He looks gorgeous today, and I instantly feel another wave of disgust at my own body.

Mom stands and throws her purse over her shoulder. “Ready?” she says, turning to me.

I nod, though I’m not ready. I stand up slowly and follow behind Mom, as we walk toward Dr. Anderson. He smiles and my stomach turns.

“Good to see you guys. Come on back,” he says, welcomingly.

The waiting room door closes behind us, as we follow Dr. Anderson into one of the rooms. Little white-noise machines pepper the hallways and desks belonging to doctors and therapists. Their purpose is to set a calm environment, but I only find them to be stressful. We walk into an exam room with two chairs, a machine to check blood pressure, a mini counter holding jars of cotton balls, swabs and bandages, and… a scale.

“Alright, do you mind taking your shoes off and stepping on the scale for me?” Dr. Anderson says simply, as if he hasn't just made one of the most terrifying requests someone could ask of me. With all of these people around? All someone has to do is peek in the doorway and look at the screen on the scale. I hesitantly slip my shoes off and walk over to the scale. I take a deep, shaky breath, afraid I might even start crying.

"Diana," Mom whispers, calmingly, "step on the scale, sweetie."

I feel my hands shaking and my lip twitching, as I place a foot on the scale, then the other. I scoot my toes up until I'm in the middle of the scale. I close my eyes, sucking in as much air as I can without it being noticeable. The feeling of wanting to disappear takes over my mind. The scale beeps, and I know from my last appointment that means it's got my weight locked in on the screen, for all to see.

I open my eyes hesitantly to see the screen.

It reads sixty-two pounds (37.6 kilograms).

"Hey!" Dr. Anderson says, "You gained some weight, Diana! That's very good. *Very* good!"

I feel a lump form in my throat and my lower lip quiver.

I’ve gotten fatter.

My god, I’ve gotten fatter.

Disappearing

"Diana," Mom says hesitantly, as she reaches to place a hand on my shoulder, "did you hear the doctor? He said that's very good. It's not a bad thing at all. That's *very* good that you're on track to getting to a healthy weight."

Her words sound so far away. Everything feels so far away. Everything except the bright screen of the scale, staring in my face, feels so far away.

I cry.

The world around me feels as if it's a dream.

No, not a dream, but a nightmare.

A nightmare where I've gained weight and everyone can see it. Everyone can see what the scale reads and there's no way for me to hide it.

I feel Mom's warmth around me, yet she still feels far away. She's saying something, but I can't listen right now.

"Maybe we should go ahead to my office," I hear Dr. Anderson's voice in the background, beyond my crying.

Mom quickly grabs my shoes and guides me through the hospital hallways, while I keep my hands over my face. All I can think about is how much I want to disappear.

Once we make it to Dr. Anderson's office, Mom sits me on the couch then sits herself next to me.

"Diana," Dr. Anderson says gently, as he sits in his office chair across from us, "can you tell me what you're feeling right now?"

I'm feeling like I've gained weight; like I've gotten fatter. I feel like I should have eaten less this week. I feel like I look absolutely pathetic right now.

I am pathetic right now.

I'm crying over something I can totally control. Over something that wouldn't have happened if I were just more careful about what I ate this week.

I blink away just enough tears to look down at my body. I put my hand over my belly. I can *feel* the extra weight I've put onto my already fat stomach.

"Diana, stop," Mom says.

"No, no, it's okay," Dr. Anderson interjects. "Diana, do

what is most comfortable for you right now. However, I want you to tell me how you're feeling about seeing that scale today."

The room is silent for a moment, as I focus on my breath, in an attempt to stop crying.

"Take your time," Dr. Anderson says, quietly.

Breathe in... and out... In... Out... In...

I close my eyes and take one last deep, shaky breath, then open them. I look at Dr. Anderson with a tear-stained face and red, glistening eyes. My pathetic face can't even compare to his perfect one.

"I used to be skinnier than this," I sniffle quietly.

Dr. Anderson nods understandingly. "Do you think that could be because you're growing?"

"I don't know," I say, feeling defeated. "All I know is what I see in the mirror."

"Do you think what you see in the mirror is you?"

I'm quiet for a moment, considering the question.

"Whether it's me or not," I say, "I find it fat and disgusting, and I have to carry it around with me everywhere. *Everywhere*. I can't escape it. People aren't going to care if what I see in the mirror is me or not; they're going to stare either way. They're going to make those comments and give those looks they always do, and say 'wow' when I tell them how much I weigh, after they ask out of nowhere."

Dr. Anderson nods.

"It makes me just want to disappear," I add, quietly. Mom grabs my hand and squeezes it gently.

The appointment continues for a while longer. Dr. Anderson asks me more questions, asking Mom a few as well, before giving her some advice and a sheet he printed out from our last appointment, titled, *Understanding Anorexia Nervosa.*

I wince at the words, knowing full well that diagnosis just doesn't match me.

I've heard that anorexics have an intense fear of being fat, and while, yes, I am terrified of that, just look at me: I'm already fat.

Well, I already *feel* fat. Dr. Anderson has said that just

because I feel fat doesn't mean I am fat, so it's so-called "progress" to replace the word "am" with "feel" for now.

Once the appointment is over, Dr. Anderson stands and shakes my hand, as well as Mom's. We're left to walk down the hallways on our own and out the exit door. The only sound in the hallways is the buzzing of the white noise machines. Mom mumbles something, but I can't hear her.

"What?" I say.

She sighs. "What you said back there," she says, "I don't think you want to disappear."

Oh, yes, I do.

"Why do you say that?" I ask.

"You say that you want to disappear, but I think what you really want is to be found, to be seen. You want people to see *you*, not your body."

I look down as we walk, not sure how to respond, but letting the words resonate with me. We open the exit door and make it to the parking lot.

"I know you don't think you do, Diana," Mom continues, "but you have a disorder, and people often see that, and only that, when they look at you. I think I'd want to disappear, too, if it was like that for me."

Mom unlocks the car, and we hop in and shut the doors. *Guess I'm not driving,* I think to myself.

"Why are you saying all this? What are you saying?" I ask Mom.

She turns to me. "What I'm trying to say is that I see you, Diana. I see your heart, your mind, your soul… I see *you.* I mean, you're my daughter! I'm going to worry and nag you, because I see your body is skin and bones, but I just hope you know that I see more than that. I'm not just another stranger walking by, staring at how skinny you are. I'm your mother, and I don't want you to disappear. You are *so* much more than your disorder. *So* much more." She wipes a tear from her eye as she starts the car.

Everywhere I go, people stare. They stare at my body and commonly ask questions about it. Questions where the answers are nobody's business but my own. I'll be asked how much I weigh, what food I eat, and even what's wrong with me or what happened. My so-called "disorder" is all these people see. Mom is right: they don't see *me.*

Before Mom puts the car in reverse to back out, I lean over and hug her tight – something I haven't done in a long while. She feels tense, yet some of that tension releases once she realizes I'm hugging her.

I guess it may seem like a silly reminder to some – the reminder that I am so much more than my "disorder" – but when that's really all people have seen for a while now, any common sense became locked in the back of my mind, so deep that I don't think I could have accessed it were it not for Mom reaching in and pulling it out for me.

"Thank you," I say gently, as I rest my face in her soft sweater.

We let go of each other and Mom looks at me.

"What?" I say.

"Can we *please* go to China Cafa now?" she says.

I groan, yet feel like laughing at the same time, at her courage to ask such a question right now. I pause, considering the question and knowing that I'd feel bad for her if I said no.

"Can you ask for a table in the back?" I ask.

Mom's eyes light up, as if that's the best thing she's heard all day.

"Of course!" she exclaims, as she pulls out of the parking lot in an instant. "Alise is waiting there for us, anyway."

I turned to her, caught off guard. "Wait – what?"

"She's excited to see you," Mom says, with that annoying mom-smile, like she's just set up a successful playdate.

I'd normally be annoyed with Mom's meddling, but this time I feel a little bit grateful, actually. I need that extra push I didn't know I needed until now, to try and start hanging with Alise again.

For the first time in a while, I actually kind of feel okay. I don't know how I'll feel a few minutes from now, when someone stares at me in the restaurant, or when a pile of egg rolls is set in front of me and I'm expected to eat them, but I can say, at least right now, that I feel okay – I'm going to enjoy that for now.

Mrs. Walker (Diana's mom)

My excitement overtakes me when Diana agrees to go to China Cafa with me. It's been so long and I feel that this is what she really needs: just a simple moment, a moment when overthinking and the obsession with food is gone. A moment when she can truly enjoy herself and not have to worry so much about what or how much she's putting into her body.

A moment when we can all be okay.

I park the car in the small parking lot and we get out. I look over at Diana and see the anxiety forming on her face.

"Ready?" I say. "Alise is inside and we'll make sure to get a back table."

Diana nods and follows as we walk inside.

A Chinese woman stands at the counter and greets us as we walk in, taking an extra glance at Diana. My heart drops slightly, hoping Diana didn't notice that extra look.

"Three, please, for a table in the back," I say.

The host grabs three menus and nods. "Of course." She glances at Diana again. "You must be hungr—"

"Thank-you-we'll-follow-you-to-the-table-now." I say the sentence so quickly it's almost all one word. My eyes shift to Diana and I sigh in relief; I don't think she noticed the comment the host almost made. Her eyes are focused on the mini fountain which decorates the restaurant.

As a mother, it takes everything in my body not to go off on people like this host. As I said to Diana in the car, if people looked at me the way they look at her, I think that I'd want to disappear, too. I understand that her appearance may be shocking and a lot to take in, and some are better at hiding their shock than others, but there's no hiding that millisecond which pops involuntarily onto everyone's face at first. Some know better and hide the shock after that, while others don't. It seems that we run into the ones who don't know better more often; it seems that they *always* stare. They stare as if she isn't a human being. As if she's just skin and bones, and not a being who has feelings, like embarrassment or shame, when being stared at with such horrible, shocking looks.

It makes me sick to see people looking at my daughter that way – absolutely sick. She's coming to this restaurant to eat food, with her mother and her friend. *Food.* Do these people not realize what a huge accomplishment this is? Do people not realize that they don't need to make it any harder for her; as if it isn't already hard enough?

Diana's wearing a loose sweater and leggings right now. It might be difficult to notice her caved-in stomach and ribs jolting out, or all the little bumps sticking out on her spine or shoulder blades, but there's no hiding her hands and face right now. Her white, pale hands appear to display every bone beneath the skin, and they always look so cold. Her gaunt face almost appears to have no cheeks, they're so sunken underneath her sharp, protruding cheekbones. Her eyes are swimming in the dark circles surrounding them.

Anyone with eyes can see that my daughter is absolutely starving.

Diana spots Alise coming out of the restroom.

"Diana! It's been forever!" Alise says, as she starts to

follow the host with us to our table.

Diana smiles. “I know. Kind of all my fault for that – so sorry. But I’m so happy to see you.”

We take our seats in a booth at the very back of the restaurant.

“Hey, Mrs. Walker,” Alise says to me as we sit, “thanks for inviting me and making Diana go out.”

I smile. “No problem. We’re happy to have you.”

I notice a small vase against the wall at our table, with a single, bright-red amaryllis in it.

“Aw,” I say, nostalgically, “Diana, remember when your dad used to bring these home all the time?”

Diana turns her head to where I’m looking, and a slight smile crosses her face. “Yeah,” she says, “I miss the bright-red ones. He needs to switch back to those kinds.”

I laugh, happy that I’ve witnessed a genuine smile from my daughter. “I do, too. I still love the kinds he gets now, of course, but there’s definitely something about that vibrant red type that really brightens up the room. Makes them seem stronger and more alive.”

A few minutes pass by and, after ordering, and letting Alise and Diana talk and catch up for a moment, the server brings out our food.

I can tell that Diana gets a little nervous when it comes out and is set in front of her, but I've learned from experience that it surely doesn't help to stare at her, or to try putting more on her plate, expecting her to eat it all.

We all have the same size plate and we all eat together, ignoring the problems in the world for just a little bit. It warms my heart to see Diana's shoulders slowly relax throughout the meal, as we all talk, and she and Alise catch up. It's such a beautiful sight. My daughter is talking with her friend and eating food she enjoys. Oh, how I've missed this simplicity so much.

It's a moment so small yet so significant, because I think Diana needs to have her mind shut up for a bit. Maybe having this moment to look back on might make it easier for her to shut it off every once in a while, in the future.

At least, I hope so.

If not, at least she'll know now that she doesn't have to

be not okay on her own anymore. At least she'll know now that she doesn't have to disappear anymore. Not with me and not with Alise, nor even with our family, after we all learn to get through this together.

In fact, I refuse to let her disappear ever again.

I'll make sure Diana won't disappear any more, but will instead be seen for who she really is. She's worth too much to want to disappear.

Toxic *Daisies*

Annika Galloway

Daisy,
symbolizing loyalty, cheerfulness
and new beginnings.

Chapter 1

James

Present

Daisy,

Do people who are toxic *know* they're toxic?

The question has been straining my mind ever since the first time I walked through the doors of this stuffy hospital waiting room.

This waiting room – it feels like my relationship with you, Daisy: cold, stuffy, full of quiet whispers and the air feels heavy, like too many memories and tragic events have passed through it.

Yeah – so much like you, I almost feel right at home as I sit under the cold air conditioner in the hard, worn-down chair.

I gave you flowers yesterday – daisies, to be specific – and they've already made it into the trash in our house. I guess you don't like flowers anymore.

Or maybe it's just *me* you don't like anymore…

I'll talk about that at therapy today, hoping a therapist will somehow fix all of our relationship problems.

It seems that all the flowers I give you nowadays only end up in the trash.

The fake daisies in the mismatched vases, which sit at the ends on the side tables here, certainly don't help that reminder. They seem to be collecting dust.

My eyes drift to an old man and woman a few seats over from me, sitting across from each other. Maybe they're a couple. They seem to be talking to each other like they are, at least, enjoying each other's presence.

I don't think you've enjoyed my presence for years. I feel as if I'm shriveling up in my seat with just the thought of that. The fact that you've probably even been repulsed by me at times. I'm not perfect, I know – no one is perfect – but I try so hard to be, for you. I try to live up to your expectations, being that perfect boyfriend you've always wanted, but it's almost as if you have your love dangling by a stick and you're holding it up, always, just out of my reach; I can touch it, sense it's there, but I can never grab it. It's something you hold onto tight and won't give me, no matter how high I jump for the taunting, dangling stick of your love.

You still love me, I know that, but you're not willing to give me any of the love you hold for me.

I feel alone when you're next to me now. Much like this moment, when you're sitting next to me in this waiting room, silent, your head facing forward, never looking at me the way you used to. Never looking at me at all now.

What happened to us?

I look back at the two old people, who seem to match each other well. *That's* what I wanted. I wanted to grow old with someone, to be happy together, even at that point in our lives. Turns out I can't even do that when I'm young. I can't make anyone happy, not even myself. *Especially* not myself.

James

Chapter 2

Daisy

Past

James,

Mom seemed worried. *Very* worried. Her face looked tired – exhausted – and that hint of fear was in her eyes, which wouldn't look at me from across the café table.

"That's… a lot, Daisy," she said, simply but heavily.

"Well, yeah," I said, "and there's honestly probably more he's been through, but that's all that he's told me."

"Are you sure he's… stable?" Mom hesitated.

This was when I recently met you, the most kind-hearted, compassionate and caring person I've ever met, and *definitely* ever dated. It hasn't even been a full year, but we've gotten so close with each other – so connected. I guess bonding over trauma does that with people.

“What do you mean?” I said. “He’s *stable.* He’s sweet and caring. You know this, Mom; you’ve met him countless times. He’s a good person. And, just for a bonus, he even bought me daisies the other day, just because he thought it was cute that they had the same name as me.”

Mom sighed. I could tell there was more on her mind, by the way that she dodged my eyes with hers.

This is what tea does to us. We go shopping, find a café, sit down with our drinks and then the words come spilling out of us, much like the drinks spilling into our mouths. It’s almost as if our drinks have a talking-potion in them. We always catch up on everything. And on that day the conversation steered toward you, James.

“What?” I said, breaking the silence – a rare moment in our times at the café.

“James is sweet and he cares about you – I can tell that much…” Mom paused, sipping her tea, “but I just want you to know that it can be difficult dating someone who’s carrying a past as traumatic as James’s.”

I was caught off guard, and I gave Mom a strange look. I

always thought she loved you, but after this conversation, sharing a little of what you've told me about your past, it seemed as if her feelings had changed entirely. Nothing in your past was your fault. You couldn't control how your parents treated you, how little money you had growing up, or how you were diagnosed with double depressive disorder as a result of your family life – along with all the other aspects which spiraled after that. None of that is your fault, and a slight touch of anger heated my body at Mom's inconsiderate warning.

"What?" I said, with a hint of negativity in my tone. "So, should we just *not* love certain people, because they had a traumatic past?"

Mom sighed again, the patience calmly remaining in her expression. "Of course not," she said. "I'm just warning you to be careful with people who are... well... broken." She hesitated at the choice of words.

"Broken people deserve to be loved too," I said firmly, knowing fully well that term fit my boyfriend – you – well. But why would Mom say such hurtful words? I could only imagine how you would feel if you heard them. Everyone needs love, including broken people. *Especially* broken people. How else are they supposed to get put back together again? Broken things don't fix themselves.

Daisy

Chapter 3

Daisy

Past

James,

"Oh, yeah, I bought a new book," I said to you, as you picked up the recently purchased book from my bookshelf. We were sitting on my bedroom floor, going through all the books I own, many of them unread.

"Another one?" you said. "What's this one about?"

I hesitated. "Actually, I forgot. The cover was really pretty, so I didn't pay too much attention to what it was about. It wasn't in the romance section, though, so I'm pretty sure I'll like it anyway."

You smirked. "You're ridiculous."

"Yeah, yeah, I know. I buy too many books that I never read until forever later," I said.

You leaned over and pecked me on my cheek. "Nah,"

you said, "you're just setting up your own sort of wine cellar, Daisy-style."

"What?"

"You put your books on your shelf and then, when the time is right, you take them off to read, just like people do with wine: they put it in the cellar, wait until the time is right for that bottle, then take it out and enjoy it."

"Wow, so deep and poetic," I said, teasingly. It actually was, to me, but I couldn't give you that satisfaction.

"Shut up," you joked with a smile.

Another book caught your eye and you leaned forward to slide it out, a touch of dust coming along with it. "What's this one?" You examined the book further. "I thought you hated romance."

I groaned, "Ugh, yeah, that one was a gift, a while back. I'm still convinced that the person only got it for me because there's a daisy on the cover. I still haven't gotten to it, and probably never will, to be honest."

"Ah," you said, with an overdramatic, poetic voice, "it just has a lot of aging to do before it can be enjoyed."

I laughed. "Or it's just a regular, crappy romance, where the dude buys a girl a flower and suddenly they're in love, and that's literally the rest of the story."

You laughed and leaned sideways, wrapping your arms around me and abandoning the romance book on the floor. You were always good at finding excuses to hug me – which I didn't mind at all, of course.

When you propped yourself back into your crisscross position on the floor, you pulled out another book, forgetting to put the romance book back in its place. It's a pet peeve of mine, which you'll never drill into your head, despite the many times I've told you about it.

"This one looks dark," you said, examining the cover. I huffed through my nose as I grabbed the romance book and put it back on the shelf, where it will probably stay forever. You looked up from the book in your hand. "Oops, sorry," you said, "forgot." I rolled my eyes and nudged you playfully.

"So, what's this one about? Have you read it yet?" you asked, holding up the book with the dark cover.

"Oh, that one made me cry," I admitted, "I loved it."

You smiled. "Of course; you love books that make you cry. I'll never understand it."

I laughed. "I just like the depth to them," I said, "how a book can be so well written and feel so real that it actually makes you cry. That's when the book is a masterpiece."

We were quiet for a moment, as I watched you flip through the book.

"You're special, Daisy," you said, after a moment of silence.

I tilted my head and gave you a strange look. "Thank you…?"

"You just have a special heart for people with sad stories. Most people I've met in my life have avoided those kinds of people." A tone of nostalgia was hinted at in your voice.

"Oh, come on," I said, "I can't be the only person you've met that hasn't pushed you away."

"But you haven't just *not* pushed me away; you've brought me in closer, if that makes sense. I don't know. I'm just rambling at this point."

You *always* do this – or try to, at least: you open up to me, then, when you realize, you shut down. You dismiss your words as rambling or not making sense – much like others have done to you in the past.

Sometimes you do what you've learned. What you've had others do to you.

"No, no, stop," I said. "You're not rambling, you're making perfect sense. Sometimes you just need someone there, even if it's to cry with you. I completely get that."

It's words like these that still caught you off guard: kind, reassuring words. You looked up from the book and stopped flipping through the pages. "Thank you," you said, with a thousand unspoken words in your eyes.

I leaned forward and kissed you gently, knowing gentleness was exactly what your body craved, after what seemed a lifetime of only roughness.

Daisy

Chapter 4

James

Present

Daisy,

"Do you know where a bathroom is around here?" I ask you, breaking the silence between us, as we sit in the cold waiting room.

You barely look at me. "Around that corner with the vending machines," you say, with a cold roughness. That's just your normal way of speaking to me now; your normal way of doing anything with me now. Cold and rough.

I stand up from the worn-down waiting-room chair and head in the direction you pointed me in, trying to avoid looking at the fake, dust-collecting daisies sitting on every side table, which seem to grow more depressing with each glance. I circle around the corner, pass the vending machines, from one of which a man is buying gummy worms, and make it into the men's room.

I quickly do my business, but spend an eternity at the sink, staring at my reflection, which is as worn down as the old mirror on the restroom wall. I don't look like I used to. I'm older, more tired, and the chaos I constantly create in my mind is now showing itself physically, in my messed-up hair and my pale, tired face.

Oh, Daisy, is it just me or does this whole therapy thing feel like more of a hassle than a solution for us?

Dr. Burke told us to write these letters, addressed to each other but more for ourselves, yet I don't even know if you're trying this, since we don't talk much anymore. I desperately hope that you are.

Maybe one day, if we can be how we used to be again, we can read each other's letters?

That doesn't seem a likely outcome, though, after everything that's happened.

I cup my hands under the running water and splash it into my face, the splashing feeling like waterboarding, rather than refreshing. I cough as I pull paper towels off the roll and pat my face dry. I take one last look at the pathetic reflection staring back at me, then head out of the restroom.

The old woman I saw in the waiting room earlier, with the old man, is standing outside the men's restroom. She asks me if I've seen the man who was with her. The worry in her eyes is too strong to hide, even from a total stranger like myself. Apparently he's wandered off and she's lost him. I can't help her very much, Daisy, and I feel awful for it. She has that same look you used to have, when you wouldn't know where I was, or when I'd have nights when the depression was worse than others. That look of being so in love that the worry almost physically hurts, that something is wrong with your partner.

Now, I bet that if I walked out of this hospital right now, and never came back, it not only wouldn't phase you, but you'd probably watch it happen. Hell, you'd probably open the door for me.

I'm not going to walk out, though. I'm walking back to that cold, worn-down chair, by your side in that cold and dusty waiting room.

I make it back and sit down next to you, back in the heavy silence. I sigh quietly and notice your hand resting on the armrest. It looks lonely and cold. I grab it hesitantly, wrapping my fingers in yours, one by one. Your hand is limp, as if I'm holding that of a corpse instead of a lover.

You look at me, for probably the first time since we've sat down in here, but it's not a good look. You look… violated, like I've broken a rule you've set in stone in your head. Your eyes are glassy and your expression is broken. I pull my hand away and set it in my lap. "Sorry," I say.

You blink a few times, turning your eyes away from me and your head forward, not looking at me once again.

Sometimes I wonder if you forgot how we used to look at each other, and that's why you don't look at me now. Other times I wonder if you do remember, and *that's* why you don't look at me now – as if even the slightest glance at me would taint the memories of how I used to look, before we started falling apart.

James

Chapter 5

Daisy

Past

James,

The quiver in your voice broke my heart.

"I'm no good, Daisy," you said, "you deserve so much better than me."

I wrapped my arms around your broad shoulders. "Stop it," I said, "stop. You're worth so much more than you say you are."

You were having one of thosc nights again; those nights when your mind spirals into a never-ending abyss of dark memories and depression. I never realized how strong a grip your past had on you, until you revealed to me these sorts of nights.

We had recently moved in together and I couldn't have been happier, getting to wake up every morning with you lying next to me – even if we usually did have to leave for work only a few minutes later.

I couldn't admit it to you, though, but I was starting to get a little tired. I don't want to say mentally tired, so I'll just say physically for now. The late nights I'd stay up with you, to make sure you were okay, to make sure you didn't add to the scars, whether they be on your body or on your soul.

Above all, though, I wanted to make sure you knew you weren't alone anymore. I worked so hard on those nights, James. I worked so hard trying to make sure you knew you had someone there with you, to love you and let you know that I wasn't like the people in your past. I wasn't a person who would hurt you.

I'm sorry I didn't give it my all on this particular night. We had been moved in for a good few months now and, as I mentioned before, I was tired. I wrapped my arms around your shoulders, but I didn't squeeze with all the love I had, like I usually do. Tonight, I sort of just let my muscle memory do the job. And I could feel, by the way that your body didn't fully relax, that you could tell.

I promise I still loved you, *so* much, but I was tired – and I'm sorry that I keep saying that, but I really was. These nights had been occurring more frequently with each passing month, as we started getting more comfortable with each other. I think you just started loving me more, and that just made you overthink and spiral more.

"I'm sorry," you said genuinely, feeling my tiredness. I hated that you knew I was tired; it only made you feel worse for making me go through these nights with you. And knowing that *I* was only adding to making you feel worse felt worse, too.

But the only thing worse than going through these dark nights with you was *not* going through them with you.

"It's okay, James. It's okay, I promise," I said, feeling like those frequently spoken words were just a script by now. *Do I even mean them at this point?* I thought to myself, *I have work in the morning.*

Wow, stop, Daisy! other thoughts said. *Your boyfriend is literally breaking down, and you're thinking about getting up for work tomorrow.* The more tired I started growing, the more selfish I felt.

I promise I was trying, James. I was trying to make you feel better, and I feel selfish admitting that I was starting to get discouraged. It seemed that, no matter how much love I gave you, a few nights later we'd be back where we started, with your spiraling taking over again. I'd look into your eyes every time, with reassuring love, and you wouldn't look back. You were too busy swimming in your self-hatred.

"Daisy, I really am sorry that I do this so much," you said again.

I just said it was okay. Please stop saying that.

"James, it's okay," I said gently, "take all the time you need."

Please feel better so that I can go to sleep.

Daisy! What is wrong with you? Your boyfriend needs you and you're thinking about sleep!

"Thank you," you said. You used to give me a kiss after I'd reassure you. You'd give me a hug and say you appreciated me, but now I think you feel bad for making me stay up, and may even be starting to become more insecure, so you don't really do that too much anymore. It seemed like you did it as a way to punish yourself, like you wanted to kiss me, but thought you didn't deserve it, so you just started to keep yourself from doing it on nights like this.

What you didn't consider, though, is that you were punishing me, too.

I had to keep reminding myself that you were just a little broken, James, and broken people need all the love they can get. But, *damn,* you needed a lot of love.

I was trying, I promise, but it seemed like I couldn't give you all the love you needed to actually be okay. You rarely received love in your past, and I suddenly found it my responsibility to make up for that, by needing to give more love than I had. It was as if you were a terminally malnourished child, starving to death. You were a recovering patient in need of constant, urgent attention, and I was your nurse. As your love nurse, I had to give you all the loving nourishment that every person needs to be healthy – and, damn, I was running out of supplies fast, with how empty of love you were. It was like the equivalent of you having no blood in your body, and the doctors working day and night to fill you up again.

Now, I'm no doctor, but I'm pretty sure that if you had no blood in your body you'd be dead. Doctors could pump more blood into your corpse, day and night, but that wouldn't make you come back to life. I'm starting to think that it works the same for love, too; no matter how much love I try to pump into you, day and night, your self-hating heart just won't start beating again. I never knew self-hatred was so strong.

I felt so selfish for thinking this at the time, but was I too late? Had you been without love for too long? Are you just an empty, self-hating corpse that can't have a beating heart anymore?

Daisy

Chapter 6

James

Present

Daisy,

We've spent a lot of nights together. A lot of dark, dreadful nights. I used to spend those nights alone, then I found you and, although I still had those dark nights, they never seemed as dark as they were before. It was as if I had been trapped in a pitch-dark room, full of only despair, all my life, and then you – the angel that you are – opened the door to let some light in.

You showed me there was a way out – a way out of this darkness – and how not to feel so broken anymore. You showed me love. You *gave* me love – and so much of it, too.

I should have told you that, whenever I saw that you were tired, when I saw how discouraged you were, when you were giving me everything you had and I was too depressed to acknowledge it. I should have told you that you made a difference.

People love the saying, *"Better late than never,"* but in this case I have to disagree. I could tell you all of these things right now, as we're sitting in this crowded waiting room. I could tell you how much I appreciate you, and how thankful I am for you, but I'm too late.

Better never than later, I think to myself.

The words at this point would feel hollow and scripted, and you deserve better than that. They'd be a cop-out, a poor, sloppy jumble of words, which wouldn't process in your mind as thoughtful or loving, but more as toxic and cheap. It would be like a partner punching his lover in the face, then saying *"I love you."*

I can't do that to you, Daisy. After everything that's happened, after everything I've put you through, it's best if I just keep my mouth shut now, and quietly wait next to you for the doctor to call us.

The air conditioning and the cold radiating off your body

work together, making me shiver.

James

Chapter 7

Daisy

Past

James,

Why did you stop talking to me? What did I do wrong? I promise I've tried my hardest to make you feel loved. I've tried *so* hard, you have to believe me.

We live together, James. You can't avoid me forever if we live in the same house.

At the time, I remember you were taking that really difficult night class, for your psychology major. Most of my classes were in the morning, so if I didn't have to go to work afterward, I would usually get home before you. I had gotten used to you coming home long after the sun had gone down, and if we didn't have any homework which absolutely needed to be done by that night, we'd always sit and watch T.V. together. Sometimes, you'd even come home with a few wild daisies for me; you mentioned there were a few small patches of grass on campus where they would occasionally grow. Of course, after that we would usually head to the bedroom, for you to start spiraling, and it would be another long night for the both of us. But before that I still enjoyed sitting on the couch with you, watching our shows together and admiring the occasional daisies on the coffee table.

However, even those moments have started disappearing. We haven't sat on the couch together in weeks. I can't even remember the last episode we left our show on. The shriveled daisies on the coffee table haven't been replaced by new ones any time recently. It seems as if you only come home now to let your mind spiral deep into your depressing abyss. Now we skip the quality time together and get straight to it.

"Hey," I said one night, as you returned home. I set my pen and school notebook on the couch-cushion next to me and stood up to hug you. I wrapped my arms around you and kissed you, hoping to push out any negative thoughts that might be creeping up on you.

"Hey," you said, pathetically putting your arms around my waist, your mind obviously somewhere else.

I let go and stepped back to face your broken eyes. "Again?" I asked, as nicely as I could.

When you looked at me, the expression on your face was the only response needed to answer my question.

"I… I just saw something on the news today, and it reminded me of when that happened to me… before we met, and—"

"I told you to take a break from the news," I said, trying not to sound as exhausted as I was. "There are so many unresolved and traumatic things in your past, you know that hearing similar stories on the news can trigger your memories. Come on, you're a psychology major; you *know* that." My tone almost turned to begging.

"I know. I'm sorry," you said, running your hand through your hair, "you deserve better than having to go through this every night."

That was that: another failed attempt at talking to you.

You slid past me and walked straight to the bedroom, leaving me alone in the living room.

I almost started to miss our long, sleepless, spiraling nights together, because at least then you were still talking to me.

I plopped back on the couch, sighing heavily and looking at our closed bedroom door. All that energy and love I poured into you – did it achieve nothing? I was exhausted, James, but still I would have given you more if you needed it. You just had to let me, but instead you started pushing me out. You left me in the dark, deciding not to talk to me anymore, thinking I'd be happier there.

Well, I should have told you then, but I didn't, so I'll tell you now.

I'm not happy, James.

Not anymore.

I'm exhausted, and you have drained me.

Daisy

Chapter 8

James

Present

Daisy,

"Do you still want to be an archeologist?" I ask you, knowing that I need to just shut up and wait quietly for Dr. Burke, but the silence is deafening, even with people talking around us.

You look up at me, clearly not in the mood for a conversation. You nod slightly. "I guess. Why?"

I look at my shoes. "You don't talk about it as excitedly or as often as you used to."

You scoff and look away. "Well, you haven't exactly been as interested in hearing about it as you used to, now, have you?" The words are cold and sharp as they roll off your tongue, as if they could pierce right through me.

Back to silence.

I don't want to start rambling; I know you've grown tired of it, so I let the conversation end here for now. Though I need you to know that I'm sorry I took away your passion. You're still going to school for archeology – or, at least, I think you are. I don't know; we haven't talked too much lately. But I can see the passion for it in your eyes is gone, and I don't think that's because of the career. It seems more like it's because of me.

Archeology seemed to be absolutely perfect for you. You've always had such admiration and interest for other people's pasts, and all their little, broken objects. I remember you telling me that at the beginning of our relationship, when we were happy. Your eyes lit up when you talked about how all those broken things told a unique story, and therefore they should be cherished. That's why you wanted to be an archeologist.

And, of course, that's why you were with me. You didn't say that, but you didn't need to. You saw a beautiful artifact, while others saw a broken mess. It's what first drew you in: your passion for hearing my story, unlike anyone else in my past. How carefully and thoughtfully you listened, then went on to cherish and love me, deeply.

I sure screwed that up.

"You still want to do something with psychology?"

I look up from the floor at you, surprised that you're continuing the conversation.

"Yeah," I say, trying not to sound too desperate. "Yeah, still thinking about therapy, maybe."

Unlike you, I never chose my major based on wanting to hear other people's stories. I chose it wanting to figure out my own. I wanted to work out everything that's wrong with me, and hopefully fix it. If I knew how the mind worked, how trauma affects the brain, how depression works, and what the science is behind insecurity and a million more things, then maybe I could learn how to stop being such a burden. Maybe I could learn how to focus on loving you more, rather than hating myself more.

You sigh and lean back in the hard waiting-room chair, looking up at the old, faded ceiling. "Maybe you'll work here one day," you say.

I look around at the outdated and dusty waiting room. "I don't think I'll want to come back here ever again, if we make it through all our sessions."

There's a long pause between us. You cross your arms against the chill of the air conditioner and look forward.

"Hopefully you can go somewhere that makes you happy, then," you say.

"I hope you can, too," I say, back to looking at my shoes.

I hope my somewhere can be where you are, too, Daisy.

James

Chapter 9

Daisy

Past

James,

When we first met, I absolutely loved reading. It was my stress reliever, my escape from reality – even the books which made me cry. You know I actually especially loved those books.

However, since we've moved in together, and gotten so busy with work and school, reading had unnoticeably slowly started dying off for me. All of my unread books sat untouched on our shelf in the bedroom, collecting dust, as if they had given up on ever being picked up again.

I don't know what it was that day that reminded me those books still existed, but something sparked inside me, which pushed my eyes to that dusty shelf. Loneliness, perhaps. We hadn't talked in so long – not really. We'd asked each other our schedules for the week, and let each other know that we'd gotten to school safely, or that one of us picked up dinner, but the last time we had a *real* conversation had felt like ages ago.

You were at your night class and I was alone again, waiting for you to return home, only to get your nightly depressive episode and push me out again. I guess it was that night which finally tipped me, feeling lonely enough to remember that my books existed, that I could escape into a reality which wasn't as lonely as the one I lived in.

I sat down on the carpet and let my eyes scan over the spines of the books, specifically the ones I haven't read yet. My eyes stopped at one in particular: the romance book. The book I was pretty sure I'd never read, and that night I found myself pulling it off the shelf. I went out to the living room, to sit in my usual spot on the couch, and opened it.

As I read the first few chapters, I realized this would be a book that I would have hated in the past. I thought back to when we were sitting on the floor of my old house, and were going through my books together. You made that cute metaphor about how books are like wine, and some just need time for aging before they can really be good. You laughed, you smiled and, best of all, I was talking to you and you were talking back.

If I remember correctly, I think I finished that entire book sitting on the couch that night. Who would have thought that I'd ever enjoy a romance book? I guess you were right: it was just a book that needed time to age.

It was one of those books that you just absolutely fall in love with, from the moment you start reading to the moment you finish. But, at the same time, I almost wish I didn't pick up that book that night. There were scenes in the book where the couple had hard times; scenes where they got into arguments like real couples. But there were a lot of scenes where they were happy together, too.

When's the last time we've been happy together, James? When's the last time we told each other, "I love you," without it being a hollow, empty and scripted statement? When's the last time we *looked* at each other – I mean, really acknowledged each other?

It was a decision I was so sure about, a decision that needed to be made: I was going to talk to you that night. I wouldn't let you go to our bedroom alone again. Whether you felt you deserved to be ignored or not, we needed to talk. We needed to end this torturous cycle of being alone, trapped in our spiraling minds every night.

I started planning it in my head. You would come home, depressed as usual, but I wouldn't let you go into our bedroom alone again, no matter how much you were going to fight me. I'd tell you I care about you, and remind you of when we were looking at my books together, that time long ago. I'd remind you that was the time I told you I'd be that person to cry with, that I'd cry with you and be there for you. I would also tell you that I'll be that person you can laugh with, too, that if we can stop pushing each other out, then we'll be able to laugh together again. I'd tell you that we can be happy again. That we need to stop this horrible, painful cycle, because I refuse to do this any longer.

I heard the keys shift in the doorknob. As soon as you walked in I stood up from the couch and put my arms around you – something I had started slacking in, since we stopped talking so much.

"Hey," I said, as I hugged you tight.

"Hey," you said, in your usual, depressed tone.

This was usually the part where you head into the bedroom to put your stuff down, and not come out again until morning. *Not this time,* I thought, ready to block your path so you'd have to talk. I released you and let my arms fall to my side, waiting for you to start trying to walk to the bedroom.

But you didn't move.

The first thing you do is go to the bedroom. You *always* do that, every time.

Did my hug really affect you that much? Did it really make you decide to stay out for a second longer, before going to the bedroom?

I felt I'd accomplished something, for a moment. I was happy that I had made you feel a little better, for the first time in a while. But then I saw your face.

You were looking downward, a heaviness in you that

couldn't go unnoticed. I hadn't made you feel better; you felt worse! So depressed that you couldn't even make it to the bedroom. Your spiraling had dug its claws into you even deeper.

"James?" I said.

There was silence in the room – a long, heavy silence – and I suddenly didn't feel as confident about this decision to talk as I had a minute ago.

"Daisy," you said, and I heard your voice crack. Were you about to cry? You always tried your hardest not to cry in front of me.

"What?" I said, gently, "What is it? You seem more depressed than usual. Please talk to me. Don't shut me out."

You sighed heavily, putting another long silence between us. I watched your feet carefully, making sure they didn't take a step toward the bedroom, to escape talking.

"I kissed another girl."

…

What was my plan again? Everything in my mind, before those words came out of your mouth, had disappeared completely. I was speechless. Thoughtless.

I felt a pain I had never felt before. A pain that shot through my entire body and made my heart feel too heavy to stay in my chest. I couldn't think. My body was stunned, frozen. My eyes were instantly wet, as if they processed your words before my brain had even had time to.

"You… you… what?" My words felt disconnected from me, as if I wasn't the one speaking them. They were quieter than a whisper; I'm surprised you even heard them.

"I'm sorry." You didn't look at me. Your words were shaky and quiet – even sincere, it sounded like. "It was a girl from my psych class. I'd never even talked to her before… but she came up to me after class, when I was the last one to pack up my stuff… She just… kissed me. I… I don't know why I didn't stop her."

You sounded so far away.

"We kissed for a while… That's why I'm home so late… I'm so sorry."

I blinked and looked down at my phone on the coffee table, the clock showing it had been about two hours since the time your class normally ends. My mouth parted as I let out a shaky, quiet sigh.

You hesitated. "Did– did you notice I was gone? You never texted."

I had been reading. I never stopped to look at the time, or else I would've texted you a long time ago, to make sure you were okay.

I didn't, though.

You had been gone for almost two extra hours and I hadn't even noticed. You nodded sadly, seeming to realize that.

"I'm… I know you must not want to look at me right now. Let me know when you're ready for bed, and I'll come out here and sleep on the couch."

That was it. You walked toward the bedroom to set your stuff down, like usual. I watched your feet as they shifted along the carpet, closer to the bedroom door. Wait, wasn't I planning to stop you from doing that tonight? We were going to talk. We were going to make everything better. I was going to remind you of the good times, like when we used to look through books together. That I would always be there for you to cry with, when you needed it. “I…”

You turned around at the sudden sound of my voice filling the silence.

Say something, Daisy, my mind told me. You waited patiently.

My voice cracked as a tear rolled down my cheek. “I told you I would cry with you, not because of you.”

You sighed that depressingly heavy sigh you do on nights when things are really bad, then you turned around, took one last step into the bedroom and disappeared from sight.

Really? I thought to myself. *That's all? Weren't you planning on saying more?* The rest of the words I wanted to say wouldn’t come out. But it didn’t matter. You were already gone.

I sat back down and threw the romance book I had just finished across the room, as hard as I could. If daisies had been on the coffee table then, they surely would have been knocked over – but I didn’t have to worry about that possibility now. I buried my face in my hands and cried.

Why did you do this to me, James?

Mom told me to be careful of broken people like you, but I told her broken people needed love, too. I told her that for you.

I loved your broken self more than anything – even my own well-being, now that I think about it. I just didn't realize that loving someone as broken as you would eventually break me, too.

Daisy

Chapter 10

James

Present

Daisy,

As we sit in this cold hospital waiting room, I can't express how badly I want to tell you that I love you. I can't say how badly I want to tell you that I'm sorry.

You gave me everything, and all I gave in return was exhaustion and loneliness.

I'm so, so sorry, Daisy.

We're only here because of you; because you still love me so much that you're willing to try and work through all the mess I've made.

I want to try with you too, Daisy, but you know me and my insecurity, which I feel is right here in this situation. I feel that, at this point, almost everyone on the planet would agree with what my insecurity is saying right about now:

that I don't deserve you.

I'm not good enough for you. Hell, I'm not even good enough for myself.

At this point, I feel the right thing to do would be to put you out of your misery. I need to let you go. But I'm afraid I'm too selfish to do that.

I know you haven't talked about our relationship with any of your friends. You probably haven't even mentioned your friends in any of your letters to me, because I know you want to keep them out of this. You've told me before that you don't want to burden them with our problems – something I'm almost one hundred percent sure you learned from me, after realizing what it did to you talking about mine.

Maybe you've talked to your mom about all of this – I can't be sure – but I hope you've talked to someone who listens, at least. I know I sure didn't listen, because I was too caught up in hating myself.

I know you won't admit it, but you're probably hating me now, too.

I look over at you, in the chair next to me, feeling the pain you feel radiating off your body. I wince slightly.

I caused that.

A tear rolls down your cheek, but you wipe it away quickly, before anyone can notice.

"Daisy?" I say, cautiously. It's as if your name coming out of my mouth gives you pain. You sniffle at the sound of my voice, and another tear rolls down your cheek before you can swiftly wipe it away.

"James," you say, looking straight ahead, "I don't think I can do this anymore."

I want to say I'm not surprised, that I was expecting this and that it is honestly long overdue, but I can't. The shock still comes, and my mind instinctively, instantly wants to stop your words from being heard. I want to argue; I want to tell you that you don't mean it, that we'll get through this rough patch and end up better than ever.

But I can't do that to you.

At the same time, though, did you really have to choose the hospital waiting room to do this? Right before we're about to be stuck in a small room together for an hour, and forced to talk?

"Seriously?" I say, more sincerely than accusingly. "We're… we're about to have our session. Do you really want to do this now?"

"I– I'm sorry," you say, as you wipe your face with your sleeve and sniffle, trying your hardest not to cause a scene, "it just came out. Maybe we should go through the session first."

"Daisy Woffard," Dr. Burke calls, as she opens the door to the waiting room.

Could you have chosen a worse time? I think to Dr. Burke. Or maybe it's the best time – I don't know.

Daisy stands up first, then me. We walk toward Dr. Burke, who can instantly tell that she doesn't need to casually ask how we're doing.

Daisy, what's going to happen to us? I wish you'd tell me what's going on in your mind.

I think I know what you're thinking already, though, as much as I hate to admit it…

We're going to walk out of this building broken up, aren't we?

James

Chapter 11

Daisy

Present

James,

Our last therapy session just ended. Yes, James, our *last.*

Oh, how I would love to say that we had a breakthrough; that we had some magical experience, where we suddenly worked everything out and now we're better than ever. I would love to say that we had some spiritual awakening, and realized something about ourselves that we didn't know before, and now everything is solved. But that just didn't happen.

We already know what's wrong with us…

You're too insecure. I'm a pushover.

You broke me and, whether or not you meant to, I let you do it.

I never talked to my friends about our relationship,

because I already know what they'd say:

"You need to get out."

"Don't stay with him."

"Why are you still with him?"

"He's not even talking to you anymore? What a jerk."

They wouldn't understand, James. They would just see you as the bad guy.

You're not the bad guy, and you're not the good guy, either. You're the guy who always took one of my books off the shelf, then would take another before putting the other one back. You're the guy who liked coming up with cute, yet smart metaphors – one of those small, simple things I loved about you. The guy who I'd cry with, who has made me laugh, smile and feel loved. The guy who let his insecurity get in the way and who was really, *really* broken. You're the guy I fell in love with.

That's who you'll always be to me, James…

You'll be you, the guy I fell in love with.

I can't stop myself from crying right now. I know you're crying, too, but my vision is too blurred to see you.

Dr. Burke had another client to see, but she showed us to this empty office, where we could talk and recover from our session. We now sit on a couch, holding each other so we don't have to see each other's crying faces.

"I'm sorry… I'm so sorry, Daisy," you say through your tears.

"I know," I say, quietly. I do. I know you're sorry, James. I truly believe you.

But we aren't meant to be. I know that now.

Though, of course, our hearts didn't know that. Our hearts only knew that we loved each other – and our hearts still do. My heart still loves you so much, James. But it breaks every time you touch it now.

I can't be torn apart anymore. If I do any more breaking, then I might not ever be able to heal again. And I know the same goes for you.

For the first time since entering this room, I look at you. I look at your broken self, seeing every tear fall from your tired, red eyes. I feel my heart cave in.

We're going to walk out of this building not together

anymore. It kills me to admit that, and I feel more tears fall as we sit in this empty room.

"This is it, isn't it?" you say with a pained, accepting tone.

I sniffle. "Yeah… yeah, I think it is."

You nod quietly. We sit for a few minutes in silence, the only sound coming from the quiet noise machines that sit in every doctor's office, along with our shaky breathing and sniffling.

Once the heavy air around us turns to full silence, we stand up, open the door and walk out, leaving our relationship behind us in the empty room.

Daisy

Chapter 12

James

Present

Daisy,

You know very well that I know what self-hatred does to a person. It's an obsession with the self; the very aspect that disgusts someone who hates themself. The hatred grows into an addiction, getting stronger each day. And when you realize that you've been too obsessed with hating yourself to notice or care about anything or anyone else around you, your response is only to hate yourself more.

This obsession, this addiction, this *hatred* destroyed us.

Please, I know I hurt you, I know I broke you, but don't end up like me. Don't be filled with so much hate that you find yourself not being able to do anything else one day. Don't carry so much self-hatred that you someday find yourself blocked from seeing all the little things in life that matter. Please don't hate yourself so much that one day you won't have any room left in your heart to love someone else.

Please, don't hate yourself, because I don't. I love you.

I love you.

James

Epilogue

James

8 years later

Daisy,

Wow, I never thought I'd run into you. And Greece, of all places! You look so happy, so content.

Seeing you like this was the closure I didn't realize I needed until I saw it.

"James?"

I turned around at the sound of my name. My eyes widened.

"Daisy!" I said, surprised. "Wow, what are you doing here?"

"Same thing you're doing here, probably: checking out the sights."

We're at a famous tour site in Greece: the Acropolis of Athens – a trip my wife and I were able to agree on for our anniversary trip.

For the first time in eight years, you and I talked. You proceeded to tell me that you were here on a trip for work. You're with someone who loves archeology *almost* as much as you do – because no one could ever love it as much as you do, of course.

"Does he put your books on the shelf how you like them?" I joked.

You laughed. "Unfortunately, no. The other day, I came home to find *three* of my books just sitting on the floor. I'll never understand how someone can't just put them back!"

I laughed. I don't blame the guy. You were always particular about your books.

I told you about my wife. How we met in – of all places – our therapist's office. We struck up a conversation when we realized we had the same therapist, and we haven't stopped talking since.

We caught each other up on our lives, and how we're both happy. And happy for each other.

I didn't say this, because I didn't want to make things

awkward and bring up old memories, of course, but I wanted to thank you. As painfully as it ended, thank you for our relationship back then. Thank you for putting up with me for as long as you did, and for showing me a kind of love that I had never received before.

You taught me love but, most importantly, you taught me the effects of hate and insecurity. You taught me that there are no benefits to self-hatred; it does nothing for you and nothing for anyone else. It only destroys. You taught me that I needed to change – not for you, because it was too late for you, but for myself, for my wife and for my future kids.

We exchanged goodbyes again, this time much happier than the last, both of us smiling as we parted ways, returning to our lives and those we love.

Love, James

A Bouquet of Buttercups

Annika Galloway

Buttercup,
symbolizing youth, happiness and
friendship.

Past

Theo, age 7

"THEO!"

Dad. He's home!

The endless possibilities run through my head: did I leave my cup on the table again; did he trip over one of my toys? Oh, no, I hope I didn't leave one out!

Wait – did Rover have an accident in the house again? I was supposed to watch him while Mama and Dad were out. He's potty trained, but dogs can still have accidents, especially if they're not let outside enough.

Did I eat the last of the chips? I can't remember.

Or did Dad just come home angry today?

Oh-no-oh-no-oh-no – what did I do?!

I sprint to my bedroom door, close it swiftly and lock it, my breathing already growing rapidly.

The loud footsteps get closer. The doorknob starts to jiggle violently.

"Open the door, Theo," Dad says.

I back away, my body unwilling to even consider obeying Dad's order.

My eyes dart around my room. There's the window, my closet, under the bed, maybe even behind the door when Dad busts it open. My options are limited, but I need to make a decision.

"OPEN THE DOOR!"

The door's locked, but he'll find a way in. He always does.

I go through my options again, of where I can run to. I have to get out of here. I have to run away. I don't have much longer.

It's time I escaped from here.

Dad gets the door open somehow and barrels in furiously, ready to do what he always does, but I am gone.

I've found a way out and I am not looking back.

Present

Theo, age 30

The hospital waiting room is crowded today, and I'm definitely not helping that, with all the friends who have come with me. I've got Leo, Paul, Nala and Luke here, taking up much of the space – even though I told them I'd rather they didn't come.

"This is such a waste of time," Luke complains.

"Shut up," Nala says. "We're here for Theo."

"Didn't ask you to be," I say.

"Yeah, well, we're still here for you, man," Paul says.

"This wait is ridiculous, though," Luke says. "You see all these people?"

"I know, Luke. God forbid other people might need help, too," Nala says.

"Guys…" Paul says in his warning tone.

"Thank you," I say quietly to Paul, a phrase which has become automatic, given how often I say it to him. Don't get me wrong, I love Nala and Luke, but they never mix well together; it's always Paul having to stop things between them, before it gets any worse – especially in public. They love to embarrass me.

"Come on, Paul," Nala says, "we don't need Luke's negativity and impatience right now."

Luke scoffs.

"Don't start," Paul says.

I rub the bridge of my nose as I sigh. This is why I didn't want them here. But they never take the hint that some personal space might be nice for me sometimes.

Of all places, too, a hospital waiting room. I'm waiting to speak with a new doctor about all of my issues, and they really decided that this would be a great opportunity to accompany me?

My last doctor – who I've been seeing for what feels like forever, and with whom I never really made much progress – retired last week, and they all know how anxious I am to meet with a new one, for the first time in ages. It's one of the reasons why they're all here today: their form of support for the change. But that support feels more like stress right now.

I guess I don't mind Paul here, but Nala, Luke and, yes, even Leo, who's been silent this whole time, are more than welcome to leave.

If I did want anyone to be here right now, I would want Ashley. She's not a childhood friend, like everyone else here, but she's definitely a real one, for understanding boundaries and putting up with me whenever we hang out.

My phone buzzes and I pull it out of my pocket. Ashley's name appears on the screen, with a text which reads, *"Have you met the doctor yet?"*

"Not yet," I type, *"waiting room is crowded today."*

"Ah," Ashley responds, *"well, text me when you get out and lemme know how it went."*

"Will do." I put my phone back in my pocket and look ahead at the fake buttercup flowers, which sit on the side tables at the ends of the rows of chairs.

Nala sighs.

I roll my eyes, realizing she has been looking at my

phone screen. "What?"

"It's just painful – you and Ashley," she says, wistfully.

"Well, what did you want me to do? Reply, *'Not seen doctor yet – oh, I also have feelings for you?'*"

"Yes!"

I roll my eyes again. "Yeah, not sure that would've gone well."

"You always say that. You have to tell her eventually."

"I don't reckon it'd go as horribly as you're thinking," Paul comments, "pretty sure that she likes you, too, at this point."

"Honestly, though, she puts up with you a lot," Luke says.

I hate it when this conversation comes up with them. Still, at least it's better than them arguing. But, really, of all things they could choose to agree on, it had to be something that *I* strongly disagree with. Anyway, I don't care if they all agree on this, I've told them countless times that I'm not dumping that information on Ashley until I've gotten in the right headspace. I need, at the very least, to make a little progress in therapy first, before presenting my screwed-up self to her as potentially more than a friend.

"Oh, my goodness, poor girl," Nala says, sympathetically.

"What do you mean?" I say with annoyance, before realizing that she's changed the subject. We all look up to see a young girl standing next to a broken waiting-room chair, a few seats down from us. The receptionist who checked me in earlier is standing next to the girl, moving the broken chair out of the row.

"Oh, sweetie," the receptionist says, seeing the girl's embarrassment, "I swear it's not because of your weight. These chairs are old and outdated; this one was just ready to break. Okay?"

"Aw, man, she broke the chair," Paul says, quietly.

It's not me Luke is looking at, yet I can feel his judgment radiating, as he looks the girl's body up and down. "That's not healthy."

"What is wrong with you?" Nala says, growing upset.

"What?" Luke says, defensively. "Does she look healthy

to you, Nala?"

Great. Back to arguing.

"You're horrible." Nala pauses, looking at the girl. "She looks so embarrassed. I should go ask if she's okay."

Nala stands and takes one step toward the girl before I intervene, not waiting for Paul to stop her this time.

"Nala, STOP!" It's an angry, loud whisper. The kind of whisper I use in public, to try and avoid embarrassment, even though it often never works. "Sit. Down," I say through my teeth. A few people around us turn their heads at me; they all seem to shift uncomfortably in their chairs.

She sits, scoffing at me, "I just wanted to ask if she's okay. Sorry for caring."

"That's so stupid, Nala," Luke says.

"Kind of have to agree with Luke on this one," Paul says, "We all know you're caring, but you don't go up to someone you don't know, who's already embarrassed, and then draw even more attention to them."

"Oh, come on," Nala says, annoyed, "she looked like she needed help. Like she could use someone to talk to."

"Yeah, that's probably why she's *here,* dumbass! To talk to a *professional.*"

"You know I hate when you use those kinds of words, Luke," Nala says.

"Then maybe don't be stupid and I won't have to use *'those kinds of words,'* right, Leo?"

Leo doesn't answer, as usual, his tone answering for him, as if saying, "Leave me out of this."

Luke scoffs, "I can never get backed up for *anything* by you guys. I'm going to the vending machine, to see what else is around here."

He always does this. I can't ever get Luke to sit still, anywhere we go. He'll get up, go exploring in places he shouldn't, then end up embarrassing me, like always.

"Can you just *not* today?" I say.

"Come on, Theo," he says, "you can't keep me from doing *everything.*"

He's right and I hate that. He loves to remind me that I'm not in control of him, that I can't keep him from getting up and getting into trouble. That I can't keep him from embarrassing me.

Luke stands up and heads for the vending machine, a power move against me that no one else can understand, except me.

Luke

The hospital waiting room is dusty, old and outdated. Even the fake buttercup flowers, sitting on the side tables in their mismatched vases, seem to have some dust on them. I can't believe that Theo is deciding to wait here – and for hours, too. It's just too crowded today, with everyone here.

I make it to the vending machine and examine all the snack options – a simple task that Theo tried to keep me from doing. I know that he's worried. I know he doesn't want me doing anything he would describe as stupid, or something that would embarrass him, but this desire for control over me is getting ridiculous. It's almost as if he's forgotten everything I've done for him. Like he's forgotten that I've been there for him longer than any of the others – even Paul. I was the first to show up in his life, the first to be there for him, the first to help him out, and definitely the first to process his past trauma with him. It wasn't Paul, it wasn't Leo and it definitely wasn't Nala.

Theo's probably pissed at me right now, but he can be pissed all he wants; I know what's best for him better than he does, and what's best for him right now is to back off and stop trying to control everything I do.

I feed my dollars to the vending machine and click button *D3*, the slot with a perfect bag of gummy worms. My mouth waters, knowing I haven't had candy in what feels like forever, just because Theo gets so controlling. But that's just Theo, I guess. I can almost hear his judgmental voice, telling me to stop, but I push him out. Just because he doesn't eat gummy worms doesn't mean that *I* can't eat gummy worms.

The candy falls forward, into the bin, as I reach down and stick my hand inside, turning my head sideways to reach and feel for the crinkling, plastic bag to touch my palm.

Then I freeze, keeping my hand in the vending machine…

Is that…?

My eyes widen.

It is!

It's Tim, Theo's childhood neighbor, now a much older man, probably in his sixties. I haven't seen him in years, maybe even a decade, and now he's just walked out of the restroom, in the same hospital I'm in.

I swiftly grab my gummy worms and stuff them in my jacket pocket, as I stand up and move toward Tim. My mind turns off, my hands form into tight fists and my eyes fill with nothing but determined rage. Everything around me is blurred, as I set my focus on the man in front of me, briskly moving my legs toward him. He's facing away from me, walking in the same direction I'm going. This is perfect; he won't know what hit him. Man, if I could just get one good punch in—

"Luke!"

I'm stopped, feeling the arm with my tight fist being pulled back, as if it won't listen to what I so desperately need it to do right now.

Nala.

"Nala! Are you serious?"

"Ohhh, no," she says, like a mother scolding her child, "you are *not* about to start a fight in a hospital waiting room. Are you out of your mind?"

I roll my eyes as far back as they'll go and bite my lip. Leave it to Nala to show up at the worst times. She always finds a way to stop me when I'm about to do things that need to be done, and which no one else will do. It wouldn't even be a fight like Nala is probably picturing, anyway; the guy is sixty-something years old. It would be more like I punch him and he falls to the floor.

"Nala, do you not see who that is?" I say, frustratedly.

"I see who it is. Theo's old neighbor, right?"

"Duh, yeah, only older and more wrinkly and pathetic-looking now."

"Luke, come on!"

"Come on? Nala, you know what that guy did."

"He didn't do anything."

I scoff, "Exactly! He didn't do *anything*! He knew what was going on. He knew everything that went on in the house directly next to his. And in the morning, when

Theo's dad would walk out of that house for work, the bastard would shake his hand."

"Okay, okay, whatever, Luke. I still don't think Theo would be happy knowing you punched his old neighbor in a hospital, while he's sitting and waiting for his therapy appointment."

"Theo's waiting for that therapy appointment because of people like *him!*"

A woman walks by, giving me a strange, concerned look.

"Mind your own!" I say to the woman. She quickens her pace as she walks away from me.

Nala sighs. "Luke, just calm down," she says, now in a quieter tone. "Theo's still going to be waiting for that appointment, whether you punch that guy or not, so just stop. He doesn't need any more traumatic events to talk about."

"Fine," I spit, gritting my teeth.

"Thank you," Nala says, still annoyed.

We go back to the main waiting area. I grab the gummy

worms out of my pocket and tear the bag open, enjoying the sour and sugary goodness I know Theo hates.

Past

Theo, age 8

I pick the small buttercup flower from the grass and hold it up, looking at the bright yellow, shining as its color hits the sun.

"My dad calls them weeds," I say.

"Well, now you know they have a different, way better name than 'weeds,'" Nala says, "buttercups."

"Buttercups," I repeat, liking the sound of the name.

There's no park or playground near where I live, so the best hangout spot is the grassy field with the small pond, a few houses down from mine. Nala has recently shown up in my life and, as much as I love Luke, it's nice having a friend who's more positive and likes going outside with me. It's nice having someone who brings a more peaceful presence, and who likes picking flowers rather than kicking ant beds and throwing rocks at things. Of course, kicking ant beds and throwing rocks are fun, but I don't always feel like doing it. Some days I'd rather spend my time around more peaceful energy, like Nala's.

Talking to Nala feels different from talking to Luke. Luke knows all about what happens inside the walls of my dreadful home – which I'd barely call a home, if Dad is there. Nala has been filled in on most of it, but her reactions so far are the opposite of Luke's: they're calm, compassionate and they give me room inside my head to think. Luke's reactions are always more fiery, angry, impulsive and his immediate response is violence. I know both are caring responses that mean well, though.

"Let's pick a whole bunch of them and you can put them in your room, in a little vase. It'd make your room prettier and might even put your dad in a better mood," Nala says, with her positive energy.

"How would flowers in my room make my dad happy?" I laugh.

"Remember we learned in class that yellow symbolizes happiness?"

"Didn't Mrs. Barett say that it also means coward or

something, too?"

Nala laughs. "Okay, so your dad will walk in your room and see the flowers; he'll be either really happy or really scared and run away – works out either way!"

I giggle, picking another buttercup. "I don't think that's how that works but, okay, Nala."

"Whatever, we know that they'll at least make *you* happier, since you'll look at them and remember a fun memory, I guess."

"Yeah," I say, simply.

Nala and I continue picking buttercups in the green, grassy field, until we're holding a bright-yellow bunch. The sun has by now set, leaving the sky a beautiful painting, with different shades of pink and orange mixed together. The brightest color here now though is the yellow of the buttercups.

"We should probably go home now," Nala says, as we admire the sunset. "It's getting late and, from what you've told me, I don't think your dad will be happy if you're not home by the time that sun goes down."

"Oh, come on," I whine, "I'm not ready to go back."

"Maybe it won't be too bad," Nala says, with her positive, hopeful tone, "if you make it home before dark and show your dad the flowers. How could your dad possibly be in a bad mood, after you got home on time and were picking flowers?"

I hesitate. "I guess he won't be – just as long as he had a good day at work."

The sun seemed to be racing me as I rushed home, with only a few drops of daylight left to spare.

"Hey, Theo!"

I look toward the house sitting closely next to mine.

"Hey, Mr. Tim," I say, waving back at my neighbor. He smiles at me, as he leans back in the chair on his porch.

I turn, still holding the buttercups, walking up the few steps to the front door. I take a deep breath, hoping Dad will be asleep on the couch or, if I'm lucky, maybe in a good mood.

"THEO."

The warmth instantly leaves my body, sending chills up

my spine.

I turn around, seeing Dad's car pull up in the driveway, his window rolled down. I can see his eyes looking into mine.

The car is barely put into park before he throws the car door open and heads swiftly in my direction, his walking staggered and his movements uncoordinated.

"Dad," I say, surprised to see him home late. "You're–you're drunk."

"What?!" he yells. I take a single pace down the steps before he grabs my shirt at its collar and yanks me down the rest. I hold on tightly to the buttercups.

"Did–did you go to work to–today?" I stutter, looking up at him, as he stretches out the collar of my shirt with his grip.

"Of course I did. Why? You think I didn't? You think I'm lying to you?" His words were slurred and his breath smelled of the familiar scent of alcohol.

"Uh– I– no, I–"

His crazed eyes look down at my hand holding the

buttercups. "Why you got flowers?"

My eyes light up with a faint glimmer of hope. "Oh," I say, holding up the buttercups to him, as my feet stumble to find firm ground, his grip tightening on my shirt as I struggle, "I made a friend. She wanted to pick buttercups with me and she said that you might even like some."

"Those are weeds, son," he slurs. "You see me cutting this grass every damn week," his voice raises as he continues, "out here sweating and getting dirty, and you think it's a good idea to bring weeds into our yard, where they can plant all their little weed seeds and make it harder to cut the grass?"

Dad actually hasn't cut the grass in at least a few months, but I don't dare correct him. "I– no, I just thought—"

"Uh, you just *thought* about yourself! Didn't *think* about making your daddy's life harder."

"Dad, please—"

He lets go of my shirt, pushing me down on the sidewalk.

"Dad!" I drop the buttercups, feeling a stinging sensation spread across my elbow. I hold my arm, turning it over to see a bloody scrape.

"Dad!" I hold out my hand toward him, in a motion to stop him. "You're drunk! It's not as big a deal as you think it is. You're just… not thinking right now. I'll pick them up and go put them somewhere else. I'll throw them in the trash or just put them in my room, or—"

He slaps my hand away and moves closer to me, his tall, stumbling presence towering over me.

"I don't wanna see you bringing weeds into this yard again, or so help me—"

"I won't! I won't!" I shout.

He raises his hand back, pure drunk rage in his empty eyes, and I know what's coming.

"LUKE!" I scream, shutting my eyes. I don't want Nala's positivity right now; I want Luke's violence, his anger and his bravery, to stand up against Dad.

I open my eyes, swiveling my head and hoping that Luke has miraculously shown up to my rescue, whether it be with the courage I don't have to jump on Dad, to hit him for me, or even to take the beating for me.

Dad pauses his hand in mid-air. "Your little friend isn't here. What, did you think screaming his name was gonna make him appear?"

I whimper, feeling weak and defeated. I desperately look around for anything: a rock, a stick, maybe even just a handful of grass to throw in Dad's face, to buy me some time. I spot the neighbor's house, less than a few feet away.

Mr. Tim.

He's still sitting in his chair. There's no doubt he's heard our whole conversation, and definitely no doubt that he can see what's right in front of him.

"Mr. Tim!" I shout, my voice cracking.

Dad looks up, seeing that our neighbor has been watching the whole scene.

I feel a forceful blow to my cheek, and the crying begins instantly. My eyes blur from the pain and the tears. I hold my hands in front of my face, hoping to block any further hits. I look to the side one last time, toward Mr. Tim.

"MR. TIM!" I scream, louder this time, more begging now than asking.

He looks at me, wincing, then, hesitating, stands up quickly. I sigh in relief, as best I can while trying to avoid Dad's hits; help is coming. Mr. Tim is coming. He's going to help. He's going to stop Dad. He's coming now; surely he's—

He opens his front door, walks inside and closes it.

The buttercups have been smashed under Dad's shoes, and squished from me rolling back and forth, in my attempts to dodge him. They're destroyed. And I don't plan on picking anymore.

Present

Nala

"You sure it was Tim?" Paul says.

"Yes, Luke and I saw him," I say to Paul. "I had to stop Luke from starting a fight in the hospital."

Paul sighs, annoyed. "Of course you did. Glad you were able to stop that. Who knows how much trouble Theo could've gotten into?"

"That's what I was trying to tell him! The last thing Theo needs is for us to screw something up here, especially after how much we insisted that we should be with him for his appointment."

Paul and I stand in the hallway, passing the vending-machine area that leads toward the hospital garden. He's the only rational friend in the group that I feel I can talk to about these issues, when it comes to helping Theo. Luke always responds so impulsively. He's like an annoying, hormonal teenager who can't control his troublesome anger. It wouldn't hurt him to be a little bit positive or calmer sometimes.

"Okay, well, whatever happens, we *can't* let Theo find out about this," Paul says, "it wouldn't be good for him to know that his old neighbor is here. Could trigger some traumatic events for him."

"Agreed. And best we don't let Luke see him again, either."

"What about Leo?"

Oh, right, Leo. I often forget about Leo, with how quiet he is.

"Ah, probably best that Leo doesn't know about this, either," I say, "he probably doesn't even know Tim, but he's also unpredictable. You don't know Leo well either, right?"

"No one does," Paul says, as if that's common information everyone knows, "but, yes, definitely unpredictable. Let's just make sure no one sees Tim."

"Got it."

Paul and I head back to the main waiting-room area and

respect what Theo told us all to do earlier, if we were going to be coming here with him: "Sit down and please, *please* don't get up and do something embarrassing or stupid!" I think he meant that mostly for Luke, since I never do anything embarrassing to Theo, I'm pretty sure. I was the one who actually *stopped* something stupid and embarrassing from happening – that being Luke trying to punch someone in a hospital. We sit down, gesturing to Theo that he can regain some control over us now.

"Please tell me you guys didn't do anything I should know about," Theo says, worriedly.

"Nope, just stuff you shouldn't know about," Luke says, with a smug tone.

Theo groans. "Paul?" he says, hopefully.

"Nothing to worry about, man," Paul assures him.

Theo sighs in relief. "You guys know how much I *hate* it when you do stuff without me – or without letting me know, at least. I don't want this new doctor to kick me out before we even meet."

"Sorry, Theo," I say, sincerely, "we won't get up again.

We'll just sit and wait with you for the rest of the time, like you need."

"Speak for yourself," Luke scoffs.

"Luke..." Paul warns.

"Whaaaatttt? Why is it *so* awful that I got up just to get gummy worms?" Luke says, stupidly.

"Because I'm trying to eat healthier, Luke!" Theo says, annoyed. "And I don't even like gummy worms."

"Are you serious? You're so controlling, Theo!" Luke says.

"I *need* to be here and you know that," Theo says, "it's because *you* can't control yourself."

"Um, I can control myself plenty. It's *you* who needs to chill."

"Luke, *stop*!" I intervene. "You know Theo is trying to rebuild his life after everything that's happened, and eating healthy is a part of that. So, it doesn't help when a close friend like you is eating gummy worms."

"Shut up, Nala. You and Paul *always* take Theo's side, on *everything*! Your opinion is biased."

"No, my opinion just usually isn't impulsive, whiny and always negative. Try being positive and calm down, for *once* in your life."

"You—" Luke is cut off.

"Stop!" Paul says, "We're supposed to be here for Theo, and you guys have just been arguing the whole time. Can you just get along for once, while we wait for this appointment?"

"Yes, please." Theo shuts his eyes and rubs his face, stressed. "It'd be nice if everyone just stops talking and gives me some peace and quiet, until this appointment."

"Fine," Luke and I both say, in our different annoyed tones.

"Will do," Paul says, in the friendly voice he uses when he's trying to resolve conflict between us.

Past

Theo, age 15

Sometimes you need a friend who gets mad at the world with you, and sometimes you need one who helps you to see the good in that same world. Sometimes, and most importantly, you need a friend who isn't negative or positive; sometimes you just need a friend to be there for you, to give you comfort. That friend is definitely Paul.

I love Luke and Nala – they've been there for me through everything – but Paul, he listens. I can tell him the most hideous details of my life, without having to worry about him blowing up with rage at the world, or having to worry about him desperately trying to find positivity in every situation.

Today has been one of the roughest days in a while. I'm old enough to fight back when someone tries to hurt me now, but physical strength was never really the big issue.

I'm in the bathroom and Dad has just left late for work,

angry that I forgot to wake him up in time. I stare at myself in the mirror above the sink, holding a warm, wet rag on my swollen eye.

"What happened?" Paul asks.

"Well, look who's late to the party, as usual," Luke complains, "what do you think happened? That son of a—"

"Luke…" Nala warns, cutting him off.

The bathroom feels crowded with all three of them here now – or, I guess, rather my head feels crowded, with all the arguing they do whenever they're together.

It's rare having Paul, Luke and Nala all together at the same time. They don't get along too much, with their vast differences. They are completely different personalities from each other, after all.

Today is worse than other days, though, and when days are as bad as this one, they all show up, trying to offer their own versions of support and love. They all mean well, I know, but none seem to have learned yet that mixing all their various versions of support only ends with me getting a headache, rather than comfort.

"Are you okay, Theo?" Paul says, comfortingly.

"Of course he's not okay! Look at him!" Luke says with annoyance, "Theo, why can't you let me have a go at him?"

"Paul or Dad?" I half-joke, as I lean closer to the mirror, with the rag still on my eye.

"Either, at this point," Luke scoffs.

I lean back away from the mirror, taking in my reflection. My dark-brown hair lacks its usual volume and my pale skin clashes hideously with the purple on my eye. I sigh.

"Why does it have to be like this?" I say under my breath, asking no one in particular.

Nala, who still hasn't learned the concept of a rhetorical question, tries her best to answer. "Everything happens for a reason, Theo," she says with a comforting, positive tone, "All this suffering and all these hardships—"

"*Hardships*? What are you, fifty?" Luke interrupts.

"Shut up!" Nala continues, "It'll..." She pauses, as if trying to find the wording which sounds most positive, "it'll help you grow. The heavier the weight of suffering, the stronger you grow."

I put the rag down and fix my gaze on the mirror, staring hard into the empty, exhausted, blue eyes that stare back at me.

"How much growth can one person possibly do, Nala?" I say plainly, looking at the weak reflection in the mirror. "How much more weight am I supposed to hold, until I'm crushed beneath it all?"

For a moment, everyone's silent – a rare sound when the three of them are together. I can feel the tension in the air, as my eyes stay fixed on the reflection in the mirror, feeling everyone stare back at me through those reflected pools of anguish and despair. I can't stand it. I can't stand any of it anymore. In the reflection staring back – *everyone* looking at me – it's too crowded; too unbearable right now. The swollen eye, the scars, the bruises, which seem to constantly own their place on my body and *in my head…* God, if I could see the damage inside my head, I think I'd drop dead right now, just at the sight of the repairs it desperately needs.

I can't look at this pathetic image anymore.

I swing my fist into the mirror, as hard as my body lets me. It cracks slightly with the pressure, then shatters completely, as soon as it falls from the wall and connects with the tile floor.

"Whoa!"

"Theo!"

"The hell, man!"

Everyone is talking at once. I fall to the floor, holding my hand, with one of my knuckles bleeding. I throw my face onto my knees, taking deep, shaky breaths, my swollen eye feeling the sting as tears fall from it.

"Someone take control!" I hear Nala shout.

"Theo, take a deep breath," Paul says, in a less calm voice than before.

"Let me handle it this time," Luke announces.

"No, stop!" My voice cracks through my tears. I wish they'd all stop talking and leave me alone now.

"We're just trying to protect you—"

"You can't control yourself right now—"

"You're not safe with yourself—"

"You have to let us intervene—"

"This is too much for you right now, and—"

Everyone is still talking and shouting, but all at once and I can't hear anything else; I can't decipher which voice is which and who is who. My head explodes from aching.

"SHUT UP!" I scream into the air, "GET OUT OF MY HEAD! GET OUT OF MY HEAD!"

Everyone suddenly stops talking, and everything around me goes dark.

Present

Theo

"Theo Pierce?" the doctor calls, after opening the door to the waiting room. I stand up and make my way through the aisles of people waiting.

"Hi. Come on in," she says welcomingly, as I walk through the door. I follow her down a hallway, into her office, where the usual leather couch greets my eyes as I first walk in. It's the same office my last doctor had, and I'm thankful that my leather couch is still here.

I manage to quickly text Ashley that I've finally made it back, as I sit down in my usual spot, hoping I'll receive a text from her by the time the session ends. Not much has changed in the room yet, except for the few boxes which sit in the corner. This new doctor must still be getting settled in.

"Dr. Cassidy," she says, holding out her hand to me. I grab it and shake it, before she sits herself in the chair across from me.

"Theo," I say, although she already knows my name.

"So," she starts, and I feel my anxiety rise. She holds a thick, beige folder filled with papers in her lap, and flips through them casually.

"You were with your last doctor for quite a while," she states.

I nod.

"So, we won't jump into too much today, since we're just meeting each other."

I sigh with a touch of relief. "Oh, that's good to hear," I say.

Dr. Cassidy laughs, lightly. "Of course," she assures, "we're just going to go over some basics about why you're here. I promise you're not starting out fresh again." She gestures to her papers, "I've met with your last doctor and he's filled me in on everything you two have talked about, so that I'd be caught up when I met you."

"Oh, good," I say, genuinely.

Dr. Cassidy pulls out a single paper from the stack and

holds it up, to look over. “Ah,” she says, “you are the patient with dissociative identity disorder, also known as multiple personality disorder.”

“Yes,” I affirm, “it’s easier just to call it D.I.D., though.”

“Noted.” She pulls her glasses out of her pocket and puts them on, squinting closely at the paper. “Sorry, I’m terrible with names,” she laughs, “and, unfortunately for you, I need to learn five of them.”

“Yeah, sorry,” I say.

“No need to apologize. It says here that the names of your other distinct personalities are: Luke, Nala, Paul and Leo – are those right?”

I nod.

“Okay, and just to confirm that my knowledge is correct from these notes, Paul is your closest friend, Nala is the positive one, Leo is the quiet one, whom you haven’t seemed able to communicate with yet we assume probably holding a lot of trauma he wants to protect you from – and Luke is the sort of impulsive, negative type?”

“Sounds about right.”

"Are they all with you right now?"

"Yeah, it's been a nightmare trying to keep them under control today."

"Ah, yes," she leans back, "the receptionist did inform me of a few complaints from other people in the waiting room today. I was told by your last doctor that's a normal occurrence."

I sigh, "Yeah. People get kinda freaked out when they see a guy talking to himself, having a conversation they can't hear the other side of."

"Well, don't think for a second that I'm going to let you get kicked out of here. I know that's what you're worried about."

"I know the complaints were probably *really* bad today, though, right?" I wince.

Dr. Cassidy hesitates, "There was one patient who mentioned they were too afraid to get a snack at the vending machine, because a man there seemed to be arguing with himself."

I sigh, annoyed, knowing exactly who Dr. Cassidy is

talking about; Luke and Nala must have been arguing again.

I wish Ashley had come with me. It would have helped having another person with me who wasn't in my head, and whom others could actually see. I would have asked her, if I didn't feel like it would have burdened her.

"I was never at the vending machine," I say, "it was probably Luke and Nala. Luke pushed me out and took control, to get up and get candy, even though he knows I'm trying to eat healthier."

"You're stressed, Theo." Dr. Cassidy crosses her legs. "You know that when you're stressed or in a stressful environment, your other personalities will come out and try to control you, as a form of trying to protect you. You were changing doctors today, and there might be other factors you don't know about, which could also add to why you've switched personalities so much today."

I scoff, "Well, their idea of trying to protect me has kinda turned more into screwing up my life."

Dr. Cassidy is quiet for a moment, appearing to analyze

me. I shift uncomfortably on the leather couch.

"The hell is she doing?" I hear Luke say.

"Shut up!" I say to him.

"Excuse me?" Dr. Cassidy says.

"Oh, sorry, no, not you," I say, feeling my cheeks turn red, the freckles on my face probably becoming more noticeable. My last doctor was used to this, but I know Dr. Cassidy isn't yet. She stays quiet, waiting for an explanation.

"Uh," I say, "Luke was just wondering what you were doing."

"Ah," she says, leaning forward, "sorry, I was just thinking of how to word what I was going to say. I know your last doctor was able to meet Luke, Nala and Paul, and it's gotten a little bit easier bringing them forward to talk with them. I was wondering if I could meet them… if they'd be willing."

"Oh," I say, not sure what to think, "it depends. Sometimes they'd rather not talk to other people, and sometimes that's all they want to do. It's kind of unpredictable."

"I can talk to her," Paul offers.

"No," Luke opposes, "let me do it. You won't do it right."

"How will I not talk to her right?"

"I've known Theo the longest and I've lived through the trauma with him, unlike *you.*"

I look at Dr. Cassidy. "Well?" she says, as if she's just said something.

"What?" I say, confused. "Sorry, Paul and Luke are arguing; I couldn't hear what you said."

This is so embarrassing.

"No worries at all. I said that, if you don't mind, we could give it a try. I'm a trained professional and this is a controlled environment."

"What if they completely shut me out, though?" I say, worried. "I don't mind too much if they have a little control and keep me in the light, so that I can be aware of what's going on, but I don't want to completely black out."

"It's for your own good," Luke warns.

"If it were for my own good, I wouldn't be in a therapy session right now," I argue.

"Hey, Theo," Dr. Cassidy says, "I don't know what they're all saying to you, but if they're with you right now and talking to you, it seems that they're easily accessible for me to talk to. Now, you know that the goal is to merge your personalities back into one – that being just Theo – but to do that I need to know as much information as I can, in order to help you. If one of your personalities is willing, let me talk to them and get more information you might not have."

I sigh. If I give up control of myself now, it will most definitely be Luke who takes control next, and he's the last personality I consider a likable one. But I know there are things Luke knows that he hasn't told me. I know there are things all of them know, which they try to keep from me.

I hate switching. I mean, who wouldn't hate giving up control of their own body and mind? But I've switched countless times today already, so what's one more?

"Just let it go, Theo. Let me talk to her," I hear Luke say.

“Okay,” I say, both to Dr. Cassidy and Luke. I stop fighting Luke in my head.

He takes control instantly, pushing me out and making everything go dark.

Dr. Cassidy

When people who suffer from D.I.D. switch personalities, the change in being is often not as dramatic as movies and stories portray it to be. Many of the alternate personalities will even try to blend in with what the host does – in this case, Theo – in order not to cause a scene and attract too much attention. This is what I was expecting.

However, I can already tell that Theo is a special case. His alters don't ever seem to get along; they fight constantly and don't seem too concerned about causing a scene in public. No wonder Theo gets so stressed, even just by one of his alters simply going to the vending machine for a snack.

Theo changes his posture. He leans back into the couch, spreads his legs and places his feet flat on the floor, in an attempt to look relaxed and make himself appear taller than he actually is. He runs his hand through his dark hair, making parts of it fall back into his face, then crosses his arms across his chest. His resting facial expression changes, appearing less friendly and more annoyed by everything. It doesn't seem that I'm talking to Theo anymore.

"Dr. Cassidy." His voice is set in a deeper tone.

"Hi," I say. "Who am I talking to, now?"

"Luke."

I've never had a patient quite like Theo before, and this is going to take some getting used to – as well as some convincing; I find myself skeptical that I really could be talking to another personality, completely separate from Theo, despite my notes and conversations from his last doctor. I bite my lower lip, feeling awkward that I'm somehow greeting a person different from the one I've just been speaking to.

I am aware that his disorder is genuine, according to his last doctor, but I haven't gotten to know Theo well enough yet to know how he works. Does he ever fake switching? Is it really possible for him to switch as easily as this and, if so, how often? Is he really that stressed today, or is he just trying to give me what he thinks I want, in order for the session to go by faster? I can't be sure, but I'm intrigued to find out, regardless of the answers.

I lean forward. "So, you're the first personality that came into Theo's life, correct?"

"Yeah," Luke says, "*I* was the one that protected him the most. Way more than Nala or Paul ever did."

"All of you showed up to protect Theo. Why do you think that you've protected him more than the others?"

Luke sits up. "Because *I* was the one that took all the beatings for him," he says, defensively. "I showed up for him when he was just seven years old. He couldn't find a way to escape his dad, so I helped him find a way."

"So, Nala and Paul have never been the personalities in control when Theo would be abused?"

"*Never*," he spits his words like acid, "Paul would show up *afterward.* He'd be the one to comfort Theo and be his little buddy, while I'd get tossed aside as soon as the beating was over. Nala would be there when Theo needed some positivity, and some kind of out to give his dad, so he could have some sense of hope that things would get better

– which they didn't, by the way."

"Wow," I say, taking in his words, "and what about Leo? There's not much in my notes about Leo."

"Leo doesn't ever talk to us. I think he showed up after me, though I can't be one hundred percent on that."

"Did the last doctor ever meet Leo? It doesn't say in my notes if he ever did."

"Man, I don't know. Probably not. You'll have to ask Theo that. It doesn't matter, though; if you ever somehow got him out, to talk to him, the guy would be a brick wall – you can't get anything out of him. Believe me, I've tried."

"*You've* tried? Or Theo?"

Luke scoffs, "Theo doesn't want any more personalities fighting in his head. If anything, he's tried to keep Leo as far away as possible." Luke leans forward, as if he's about to whisper a secret. "But, yeah, I've tried. I'm the only reason we even know Leo's name. We've talked some, but as soon as I ask any questions about him… he shuts up."

I pause, writing down what Luke tells me. "So, does Theo know that you've tried to get Leo closer to you guys?"

"No," he says, "but I don't care if you tell him; he's mad at me all the time now, anyway. The *real* stuff, that he can't *ever* know…" he shakes his head slowly, "you *know* I'm not about to tell you."

"Why?" I say, although I know the answer.

"You're his shrink!" Luke laughs, obnoxiously. "You'll tell him everything I say, as soon as we switch back to Theo. Say, how does confidentiality work when the person has D.I.D.? Can I sue you if you reveal anything I say to the other personalities?"

"Good point," I say, "but, no. Treatment – especially for D.I.D. – is, you know, supposed to work best when things *aren't* kept from the patient."

"That's what you think, but you have no idea what you're doing," Luke snaps. He scoots to the edge of the couch, his expression cold and hard, looking directly at me. "Why do you think we all made sure to be with Theo on the day he's getting a new doctor? You think that attempting to merge us all back together, into one person, is what's best for Theo, but all you know about him is on those little scraps of paper with the messy handwriting. You don't know *anything*, and we're here to make sure you don't screw anything up for him. He's here to talk about his problems, not to get *more* problems," Luke scoffs, his words spitting venom.

"And that's what trauma does. Theo thinks he knows most of what his dad put him through but, hell, if he actually knew *everything*," he emphasizes, "he'd walk outta here and keep walking, 'til he made it onto the interstate, in front of a car going eighty an hour."

I let silence fill the room for a moment, feeling the tension settle in. I wait before responding, wanting to make sure he's finished with his rant.

"But, yeah," Luke says awkwardly, leaning back into the couch, "just had to talk to you, to make sure you know who *really* protects Theo. *And* to make sure you stick to only talking about the problems he's aware of, not adding any more to the trauma list."

"Luke," I say, concerned, taking off my glasses. I speak

slowly and clearly, hoping I can get through to him, "Theo's memory is filled with massive gaps. I understand that you're trying to protect him from his past trauma and problems, but it has come to a point where it is *you* who is causing Theo's problems now."

Luke's lips part and his eyebrows knit together in disgust. "Excuse me?" he says in disbelief.

"I'm not saying this to offend you—"

"Then why the hell are you saying it, because you definitely aren't saying it just to tell the truth?" Luke accuses.

"Luke," I say his name again, trying to remain professional and not raise my voice, "just think about today, for example, how incredibly stressed he was because he didn't want to switch, and how worried he was about causing a scene or even getting kicked out of the hospital, because of the behavior of his alters."

Luke rolls his eyes and scoffs, "Oh, are you *kidding* me? I get up to get a snack from the vending machine, and all of a sudden *I'm* the one causing all of his problems now?

Cassidy, come on! He's just so *incredibly* controlling!"

I flinch slightly at the sound of my last name being used without the title "Doctor," but I remain calm, my voice staying level and sincere. "Do you really think it's fair that Theo has to share his body with four other, completely different personalities? Can you imagine for a moment how hard it must be for him *not* to be controlling his own body? What it must be like to *try* not to control his body when others are intruding in it – and in his mind, as well?"

Luke's eyes widen. He stands up quickly and suddenly, his hands balled into tight fists at his side. I scoot back in my chair, sitting up and quickly putting myself on guard, at the sudden and drastic movement. His posture makes him appear taller than Theo, despite the two being in the same body.

"Intruding?!" Luke says, infuriated and taking full offense at the term. "So… what, was I *intruding* when I was getting beat up constantly by his dad, instead of him? Was I *intruding* when I'd stand up for him and hit back, whenever he was too scared to? Was I *intruding* whenever

I'd protect him from seeing all the things that'd screw him up even more or hurt him, like earlier, when I saw that bastard neighbor of his?" He breathes heavily, his nostrils flaring with rage and his widened eyes looking intensely down into mine.

I ignore his anger for a moment, caught off guard and surprised by the sudden revelation of information. "Neighbor?" I say, with a tone of confusion.

The rage in Luke's eyes leaves them for a second. He takes a shallow breath in, his facial expression changing from purely offended to a barely noticeable tinge of fear, before turning back quickly to angry.

"Luke," I say calmly, taking a deep breath and keeping my guard up, my body tensing in preparation for whatever may happen next.

He continues standing over me for a second longer, then, in one swift move, turns around, aggressively swings the door open and storms out, slamming it shut behind him.

I let out a shaky breath, hearing his heavy footsteps grow quieter as he moves farther down the hall.

Paul

"Since when do you want to talk to me?" I say, confused that I've so easily been given even an ounce of control from Luke.

"I screwed up. Man, I really screwed up in there," Luke says.

"What? What's going on? Why are we walking down the hall? The session's not over yet, is it?"

"I told the doctor about seeing Tim in the waiting room," Luke admits.

"What? Why would you do that?" I say, taken aback by the information.

"It was an accident! She got into my head."

I'd maybe expect this from Nala, but Luke? Since when does Luke give people information they want? Since when does Luke give people *anything* they want?

"Luke, we have to go back in there," I say sternly, as he keeps walking. "Don't you dare walk back into that waiting room."

"We can't go back in there," Luke says, talking quickly and frantically. "Theo will find out and then he's not gonna leave the room, knowing there's a chance he'll run into Tim. Then he'll have a panic attack and… Paul, I can't deal with that; I can't be the reason Theo has another panic attack. I can't let him find out about this – I just—"

"Luke, Luke, calm down," I interrupt him, his words becoming too quick to follow. He's breathing hard, his breath growing shallow. "Luke, you're going to have a panic attack from thinking about panic attacks, if you don't calm down."

Luke has stopped walking and is now leaning against the wall of the hallway, trying to catch his breath slowly, while holding his chest.

"Luke, I need you to calm—"

"Stop saying my name so much! I'm not a child!" he interrupts.

"Okay, okay, sorry," I say, calmly, "just take a deep breath. Listen, it's not like it's his dad that you and Nala saw; he probably won't freak out as much as you're thinking he will. Tim was a horrible guy, but it wasn't him who ever actively did anything bad to Theo."

"Paul, you're acting like Nala right now, with how stupidly positive you're trying to be. The guy would sit outside and *watch* it happen. He'd listen to screaming almost every night, like it might as well have been crickets." Luke sniffles like he's trying not to cry.

I sigh, not sure how to respond. "Well, what do you want to do? We can't go back into the waiting room like this and we can't just stand in the hallway."

"I don't know," Luke whines.

"Let me go back in there and talk to her. You can't handle this right now." *You think I won't talk to her, after that catastrophe of yours in there?* I think to myself.

"Fine," Luke spits, frustratedly. "Whatever. Go."

Luke gives up control – a rarity for him – and I take it, as we turn around and head back to Dr. Cassidy's office.

Theo

I'm in my car in the hospital parking lot, sitting in the driver's seat with my hand on the key, having started the car.

"Guys…" I say, preparing to be furious, if they did what I think they did, "why am I in my car?"

I'd better be wrong.

No one answers.

"You guys can't be serious! Hello?" I say to the empty car, growing frustrated.

"For the record, I had nothing to do with it," I hear Nala say.

"Nala, come on, shut up!" Luke says, annoyance in his voice.

"GUYS!" I say, refusing to let another argument play nonstop in my head. "Did I really get almost *no* time with the new doctor? Last I remember, I was going to let Luke talk, since he was fighting me so hard on it."

"I swear I didn't talk the *whole* time," Luke says, defensively.

"Dr. Cassidy needed to talk to me," Paul clarifies.

I pause, not even sure how to respond to such a stupid comment. "*I'm* the one that Dr. Cassidy needs to talk with. *I'm* the one who's her client. You can't be serious, Paul! *I'm* paying this doctor and all I got was about five minutes with her!"

"Yeeeaaahhh… I don't know about this new doctor, Theo," Luke says, with his annoying, skeptical tone.

"As surprising as it is, Luke is kind of right on this one, man," Paul says, "we just weren't sure what to do. Dr. Cassidy had some catastrophic ideas, which could cause you a lot of trauma if we carried them out, and it was best if you didn't hear them."

"The hell?!" If they weren't a part of me, I think I'd punch them right now. "She's a doctor! You guys can't protect me from everything forever."

"Come on, Theo, trust us on this one," Luke says. "If she got it into your head that it'd somehow be a good idea, and you ended up actually doing it, you'd just be revisiting your trauma."

"What was the idea?"

...

Silence fills my head, and I briefly wonder where this silence was when I needed it in the waiting room. I most certainly don't need it now. I need answers.

"Guys?"

Nothing.

"You can't keep doing this to me!" I shout. "You guys can't just keep shutting me out and trying to protect me like this!"

I let my head fall on top of the steering wheel, exhaling heavily with frustration.

They used to help me. Luke went through everything for me, taking all the pain yet still having the bravery I didn't have to stand up for me, even when he knew what it would lead to most of the time. Paul was the guy who could comfort me through everything. He was always there for me, listening to every last problem I could possibly think to talk about. Nala would always be there, whenever I needed a reminder of the good in the world. She'd always be there when I needed a sense of hope – when I needed to see beauty in the ugliest places and situations. Even Leo, who I've never gotten to know too well… but I think that's just his own way of showing that he cares. I know he's gone through a lot – maybe even worse than Luke – but he keeps a distance from the rest of us because of that; he keeps his own traumatic experiences as far away from me as possible, refusing to ever talk about them, in hopes that I'll always be protected from even the slightest chance of remembering them.

But, now?

It feels like all they do is sabotage me, and they can't seem to understand that concept. They think they still need to protect me. That's what they came into my life for, after all, but what they can't seem to realize is that the longer they try to keep my past from me, the more it's going to follow me – for the rest of my life.

I lift my head back up, sighing again and looking out

into the hospital parking lot.

I gasp, taking a quick and sudden breath at the unexpected jump-scare which just appeared in front of my car. It's Mr. Tim, my childhood neighbor. Decades later, I could still recognize that face anywhere. He's walking across the parking lot, clear as day, strolling in front of my parked car as if nothing's wrong. As if he's never caused anyone harm or pain in his life.

I feel my head burst with a headache, like I'm suddenly being pushed from my own mind again. I grab my head and groan, feeling a forceful push to black out. My heartbeat grows quickly, beating faster with every push I feel in my head.

"St—STOP!" I manage to shout to everyone in my head, knowing exactly what they're trying to do.

"Stop fighting, Theo!" Luke warns, aggressively, as the urge to dissociate and black out pushes harder.

I look back out of the front window, wincing and still holding my head.

He's noticed me.

Mr. Tim is looking right at me now, and my breathing spikes in its shallowness, the air around me growing heavier and harder to grasp.

Luke, Paul and Nala are all talking at once, causing a panic in my head.

"LET GO, THEO!" Luke shouts in my head. I can feel how pissed he is at me for fighting him over control.

"I'm fine!" I say sternly, pissed at all of them. I've had enough of them today.

Mr. Tim and I make eye contact, and I know he's recognized me. Who wouldn't recognize the same eyes which begged for help all those years, when nothing was ever done to help the person behind them? The eye contact is brief and lasts for a millisecond, but I know both of us have a thousand thoughts racing through our heads for that brief moment of time.

Mr. Tim blinks and continues walking, quickening his pace to get out of the way of my car. My breath returns as I take a deep, shaky gulp of air. My hands are shaking, my mouth is dry and everything around me is painfully quiet.

Then my headache dies down and my head is soundless. All I can hear is my breathing, quietly filtering in and out of my lungs.

Everything is silent.

“Whoa…” I hear Luke say quietly in my head.

Nala hesitates. “What just happened?”

“Are… are you okay, Theo?” Paul says.

They’re all shocked, and for once I feel like we’re all the same person, feeling and thinking the exact same thing.

I just saw a living, breathing, walking reminder of some of the worst trauma I lived through in the past… and… and I think I’m okay.

“I’m—I’m okay,” I answer Paul.

They’re all silent, but I know they’re still there. I take a deep breath, put the car in drive, and drive out of the hospital parking lot.

I drive in silence, enjoying the rare sound, and keeping the music that normally plays shut off. I listen to the quiet hum of the car’s engine as it moves down the road. I stop at a red light, hearing nothing but my very own, quiet thoughts in my head.

After a moment, I hear the quiet voice of Paul, "Why didn't you let us protect you?"

"Because I can't keep running," I say, simply and quietly. "The longer I run, the longer it'll follow me."

Another moment of silence.

"You almost had a panic attack, though," Luke says, with a rather more worried tone than his usual aggressive one.

"But I'm okay, aren't I?" I say. I sigh, taking a deep breath as the light turns green. "That's what I've been trying to tell you guys: you can't protect me forever."

Their job is to switch whenever I face any situation which could be terrifying, stressful, uncomfortable, or anything, really, that could remind me of my past – but these situations are a part of life. For me in particular, a lot of these situations *are* life at the moment, and no amount of switching from personality to personality will avoid them forever. I'm going to have to face everything at some point, and I've decided that I'd rather it be me who chooses when that point will be, rather than other factors. If it's not me choosing when it'll be, chances are it's all going to come bursting in, when I least need it to.

I'm not running anymore.

"Guys," I say firmly, "what was Dr. Cassidy's idea?" It's more of a demand than a question, an order to stop them keeping things from me, now that they've seen I can handle more than they think.

...

Another moment of silence. I can feel them hesitating in my head.

"She… she wanted you to visit his house…" Paul says, quietly.

"Dude, shut up!" Luke says in a loud whisper – as if whispering in my head will do any good.

"Dad's house?" I say, surprised. "I can't see him again. That wouldn't be facing fears; that would be facing death – or, at least, something near it."

I'm honestly disappointed. I thought Dr. Cassidy would have something better; an idea that was good, and something healthy for me to try. But, facing my dad? That's just dangerous, and there's nothing healthy about it.

"Exactly," Luke said, "so don't even bother. We told you it was a bad idea that you wouldn't need to hear."

"You wouldn't be facing your dad, Theo," Nala says.

"Will you two shut up?! What is wrong with you people?" Luke says.

"What?" I say, confused.

"Theo, your dad's in prison," Paul explains. "Dr. Cassidy looked up his name and there's no possible way he's ever making it back to that house, nor anywhere else that doesn't have barbed wire surrounding it."

"My dad's in prison?!" I say, surprised, although I shouldn't be. "Who's living in the house now, then?"

"She doesn't know," Nala says, "but apparently that neighborhood has been advertising a huge yard sale next weekend, which a lot of houses there are participating in. She says it'd be a great opportunity for you to go and maybe walk around the neighborhood… and eventually, slowly make it to your old house."

"Eh…" I hesitate, "I don't know. A neighborhood yard sale would make me look less suspicious than staring at someone's house, I guess, but it'd also mean that there's a lot of people there. A panic attack already sucks enough, without people there to stare at you."

"Like I'm saying," Luke argues, "you can't handle it, Theo. Don't get too confident, just because you survived one tiny event. And what if Tim still lives next door? You think you can handle seeing him *plus* everything else? There's probably still bloodstains on the sidewalk to your house."

"Well, Dr. Cassidy doesn't want you going alone," Paul says, "she wants you going with a friend that's… you know… not a part of you… in case anything happens."

"Like Ashley!" Nala says, with a hint of excitement.

I pause, considering every possibility of things that could go wrong or right. It feels like this could be the most dangerous exposure therapy ever attempted – not because of external events, but because of internal events that might occur.

But exposure therapy is known to be pretty successful, as long as it doesn't go too far…

I hit another red light and pull out my phone, in hopes that a text from Ashley will appear on the screen.

"How did it go? Are you ok? Anything I can do to help?"

She sends multiple questions in a text like that when she's worried, and I feel a tinge of guilt that I forgot to respond as soon as I got out.

I've done nothing to help myself for years, and I've only felt myself grow worse, more terrified of facing the past. So, traumatic experience or not, I know I'm only going to continue feeling worse if I don't try anything to feel better. I might as well try this.

I take a deep breath and respond to Ashley:

"I'm ok. I'll give you more details later..."

I pause my typing, not sure how to word what I want to say…

"...and I think there's something you could help me with if you're up for it."

I press send.

“Yayyy!” I hear Nala cheer.

A little over a week later.

The houseowner

The neighborhood's annual yard sale couldn't have been on a more beautiful day this year. I've got every table and item of clothing set up perfectly and neatly in the driveway. My husband has already begun walking around the neighborhood, to see if anyone is selling anything we want, and the kids are running in the yard, picking some of the hundreds of bright-yellow buttercups that flood the lawn around this time of year. We're the only house I've seen in the neighborhood so far that grows this many, and the kids are always proud of it.

"Mama!" Tara, my youngest, shouts. She races up to the table I've sat down at and throws a bouquet of buttercups in front of me. "For you," she says quickly, before running back to play in the yard with her brother, small strands of hair sticking to the sides of her face with sweat, not a care in the world.

"Thank you!" I say, with an emphatic and excited tone. I pick up the buttercups from the table. A few of them are missing petals, some appearing a little squished and damaged from Tara holding onto them too tightly with her tiny hand, but they are beautiful, nonetheless.

Numerous people walk along the sidewalks, stopping from house to house, to search through the boxes and tables of used items people have set out for sale. A few stop by my house, and I sell a few clothes and old toys the kids no longer play with. I think the turnout is better than last year; the annual yard sale seems to grow more popular every year.

I mostly leave whoever stops by my driveway alone, letting them shop on their own but answering any questions they ask. I lean back in my chair and catch up on a book I've been meaning to read, letting the sun in the cloudless, blue sky hit its crisp, eggshell-colored pages, while vaguely hearing the chatter of people passing by and the kids laughing, as they run around in our yard beside me.

"It's going to be okay," I faintly hear a woman say, as

her voice comes into earshot.

I look up from my book, seeing what looks to be a couple slowly making their way toward my house. The man with her is holding his hand to his chest, while the woman holds his arm so tightly it seems to be the only thing keeping him from collapsing. I stand up and set my book down quickly. Is he having a heart attack?

The man stops, slowing the woman as well. He shakes his head and seems to say something to her.

“Take your time,” she appears to reply.

I take a few hesitant steps toward the end of my driveway, not sure if I should try to help.

“Everything okay?” I say, after a moment of watching them struggle, raising my voice a little to make sure they can hear me.

The woman waves awkwardly. “We’re okay…” She pauses, trying to find the right wording. “He just used to live here, but the memories weren’t exactly happy, so we’re having a hard time.”

I nod, “Oh, okay. Would you like to sit down?” I gesture

toward the lawn chairs behind me.

"Yeah," the woman says, then looks at the man, "yeah, let's sit down, okay?"

The man nods hesitantly, his entire body visibly shaking.

I quickly pull the chairs up for us all to sit down, wondering in the back of my mind how a house full of such beautiful memories for me could have such a negative impact on someone else.

Theo

The house is beautiful, unlike how it looked when I lived here. Dad was right: bringing those buttercups into the yard all those years ago really did end up creating an entire lawn of buttercups – or, in his eyes, an entire lawn of weeds.

"Wow," Nala had said, when the house first came into view, "the buttercups have really taken over! It's beautiful."

"It looks like a completely different place, almost. It used to be so bare," Paul says.

I stop, feeling my heart starting to race at the sight of the house. I grab my chest while Ashley grabs my arm, reminding me that she's still here.

I feel cheated. Why is this house so beautiful now? Where was this beauty when I lived in it? *This* house, the house I always hated coming back to and always ran away from. The house where the ugliest, most hideous, atrocious events took place now has a new coat of paint, windchimes and a lawn full of bright yellow buttercups. It just doesn't match. It doesn't look right; doesn't feel right. A house so ugly, with such a violent history and tragic memories, shouldn't look this beautiful. It shouldn't look so happy.

I suddenly feel claustrophobic, even though everyone around us is at least a few feet away from me and Ashley. I feel my breath grow shallow and my head starts spinning.

This isn't right. I expected an old, rundown, broken, bare house. I expected a hideous house to match the hideous memories; a tragic scene, like I remembered it to be, almost like a graveyard. I felt that maybe I could handle that. But, this? A beautiful, seemingly welcoming house, with children happily running around the buttercups and a mother smiling and relaxing? What is a happy, lively family doing in my graveyard? I feel mocked – betrayed, almost – as if I came to visit a tragic grave, only to find that an amusement park has been built over it.

"It's going to be okay," I hear Ashley say.

The woman of the house looks concerned. As we get closer, she offers lawn chairs for us to sit down in. She and Ashley are talking now, but I can't hear anything they're saying; the sound of my heart beats too heavily in my ears.

The air is so fresh, so vibrant, yet I can't breathe it. I'm gasping for air – the familiar stale, thick air I was expecting; the air I was used to. I clutch my chest tighter, feeling as if my heart is about to burst. My head hurts and I feel everyone pushing to take control, to stop my panic attack. But I push back; I can't switch. I can't black out.

"Hey, just breathe," Ashley says, as we sit. She places her hand on my arm and squeezes gently. The woman looks concerned, and I feel embarrassed for having a panic attack in front of her.

I'm sitting in my old driveway – the driveway Dad would always park his car in. It would usually be dawn when he returned home, sometimes drunk, always angry. I could vividly hear the car door slam whenever he'd get out. This is the driveway I didn't dare be in whenever Dad was in it. The driveway I'd get thrown onto, pushed down on… hell, I'd even spent the night out here sometimes.

Now there's chalk on it: drawings of rainbows, scribbles and smiley faces.

"Theo," Paul says, in his comforting tone, "you need a break." I feel like a kid again for a moment, with Paul speaking to me like he used to back then, in his role of comforter.

I feel weak, like I'm about to pass out. I still can't take a good breath and my heart won't calm down. As I look at this house, I feel memories being dug up which I've had buried deep within me for years. They come up all at once, each one worse than the last, and becoming more vivid the longer I notice the features of the house, which no amount of paint or buttercups can hide. This paint job can't cover up the chipped, worn-down and ugly patina underneath it – not for me. This chalk can't cover up the scuffing of the driveway, or the sound of Dad's car door, eternally slamming. The windchimes can't cover up the screaming, the yelling, the sobbing and the begging for help. These buttercups can't cover up the memories.

None of this can cover up the memories.

But I can.

I feel a strong, forceful push to take control in my head –

a force stronger than Nala, stronger than Paul and even stronger than Luke. I take one last, pathetic gasp for air, and my heart stops beating in my ears, my body stops shaking and all sound disappears.

I’m exhausted. I can’t push back anymore. Can’t fight the demand in my head to be protected anymore.

I’m forced out of control, and everything goes dark.

Leo

I am a brick wall, an immovable force, an obstacle that not even Theo can get through.

The others talk too much. They slip up, spill Theo's memories – the ones he's not supposed to know about – and they're growing weaker at taking control to protect Theo with each mistake.

That's why his worst memories – his most horrific experiences, his traumas and darkest thoughts – they all go to me. They're for me to hold onto and safely lock away, and for Theo to never discover.

Yes, Luke holds a lot of the trauma, too – most of Theo's beatings belong to him, after all – but not even Luke is capable of enduring the memories that I hold.

"Theo," Ashley says, "are you okay?"

I turn my head toward her. Her face is twisted with concern and worry, while her hand is gently squeezing my arm.

Theo is better than okay. He's safe. He's calm. He's no longer trembling. No longer gasping for air. His heart isn't almost beating out of his chest anymore.

"Theo?" Ashley says, after a moment of silence.

"What's he doing?" the woman of the house asks, hesitantly.

I don't answer them. I never do.

Ashley leans in closer. "Hey," she says, quietly, "can you talk to me? Did you switch?"

I'm silent. We're not going to be talking until Theo comes back, and that's going to be when we're as far away from this house as possible.

Ashley leaves me alone, now talking to the woman and explaining D.I.D. to her, while still holding my arm and continuously glancing at me. The woman's expression grows more concerned with every word Ashley says, her posture stiffening and becoming more on guard.

I examine my surroundings, studying the once depressing and broken house, now a flourishing, safe home. The kids running around the lawn and picking the buttercups have no idea of the cost of those little bouquets they hold in their hands. My heart feels heavy at the sight, and feels as if it will cave in, but I know I've been made to handle these feelings, unlike Theo.

This house could have been beautiful all this time, I think to myself.

I suddenly feel alone. So alone. I know Theo doesn't belong here; none of us in this complicated head do. Everything is beautiful now, flourishing and alive. When Theo was here, everything was dying.

I feel out of place, like a drop of oil in a lake of fresh, peaceful water which refuses to mix with me, refuses to touch me. The beauty and peace of this place surround me, because I am in its environment, but it doesn't touch me; I can see it but I can't feel it.

It's not for me.

It was only for me when it was hideous and drowning in chaos; when it was thick, suffocating oil instead of the fresh, peaceful water it is now.

I feel myself growing bitter – angry, even – at this

surrounding beauty, which mocks me with its unreachable distance, a wedge between us. Why do these kids get to bask in the beauty and peace of this home, when I had to endure what it was like when it wasn't a home? Why am I forced to hold all the trauma from this house, while these kids get to hold the carefree memories of a harmonious, untroubled childhood? Why do—

"For you!"

I blink, realizing I have gotten lost in my spiraling thoughts again. I look down to see a little girl standing in front of me, holding up a vibrant, yellow bouquet of buttercups. My lips part and a look of awe and confusion fills my face. She's smiling, pure joy and innocence covering her expression as she holds them. She hands me the flowers and I take them.

"That was so sweet of you, Tara!" her mother says, still sitting in the chair next to me. She turns to me. "She loves giving flowers," she says, smiling sweetly and sympathetically.

The little girl runs off back into the yard, to continue

playing with her siblings. I look down at the flowers, knowing that no one will ever understand the incredible importance they have for me.

For the first time, water mixes with oil.

Theo

I'm holding buttercups in my hand.

Buttercups.

The flowers I was too afraid to touch when I was young, after what happened the last time I picked some.

I look up and process my surroundings. I'm still sitting in the chair, with Ashley and the woman who owns my childhood house. The house is still in my sight; we haven't moved.

I look back down at the buttercups.

Leo gave me control back.

I look at Ashley in confusion and concern.

"Tara gave you flowers." She gestures toward the youngest girl, still playing in the yard with her siblings. "I think she saw that you needed some."

I run my fingers across the soft, delicate petals of the buttercups, amazed at the sight in front of me.

How am I still here? I think to myself. I was fully

expecting to switch back when sitting in Ashley's car, far away from here. Never would I have expected this: to be still in the same spot where Leo took control because it was too much for me. And I certainly *never* would have thought I'd ever be holding buttercups in my hands again, after all these years.

"I don't think you need my protection anymore."

I feel my body freeze. I've never heard this voice in my head before. It's not Paul, Nala or Luke.

"Leo?" I say with confusion. He's never spoken to me before. He's always been silent.

"Theo, you okay?" Ashley says, sitting next to me.

I look to her, then the woman, whose concerned, on-guard expression hasn't left her.

"I–I think I need to go for a walk," I say, as I stand up.

Ashley leans forward, about to stand. "Oh, okay," she says, "we can go, then."

"No," I hold out my hand, stopping her, "I need to go alone."

She pauses for a moment, exchanging looks with the

woman.

"I don't think he should be left alone," the woman says cautiously, as she glances over at her kids, playing in the yard.

I look at Ashley directly, gazing into her slightly panicked, hazel eyes. "I promise I'm okay," I assure her. "Just let me walk around the block. I'll be right back, okay?"

Ashley and the woman have been talking the entire time, and I know I'm not leaving her in an awkward situation. They've exchanged questions and, although the woman is definitely more on guard than before, she is certainly interested in listening to Ashley explain my story, without giving too much information and getting too in-depth.

Ashley looks at me and grabs my hand. "Okay," she says, gently. "Don't make me regret this decision."

I squeeze her hand tightly, like she does so often to me, whenever I'm feeling panicked. "I won't," I say, then I let go and turn away, taking a step out of the driveway, onto the sidewalk of the neighborhood.

I walk until I feel I'm far enough away from everyone, feeling a sense of relief once everyone is out of earshot.

"Leo?" I whisper, desperate to hear him say something again.

He's quiet, but I know he can hear me.

"Why did you let me see the house again?"

I hear his hesitation.

"Leo? Please."

"I…" he sighs, "I just don't think you need to be protected from it anymore."

I'm silent, letting his words process. I look down as I walk, kicking a small rock in front of me.

"It's beautiful now," he adds.

I scoff, laughing sadly, "Yeah, I noticed."

"You can be a part of that, Theo."

"Doesn't seem like it."

"But you can – if we all stop trying to protect you from it."

I shake my head. "That doesn't make sense, man."

"Yes, it does," Leo argues, "Theo, I'm trying to tell you

that you're right: we can't protect you anymore."

His words sink into me, as I kick the rock for a final time before it falls off the sidewalk.

"Look, I get it now, okay?" Leo admits, "You can't accept your past and move on if we don't even let you acknowledge it. You saw a beautiful home, a happy family, a safe place – everything you wished you had as a kid, but you couldn't stand seeing it. You couldn't accept it because you haven't got the chance to move on from how that house looked before." He pauses, "Look what's in your hand."

I hold my hand up, noticing that the bouquet of buttercups is still being held safely and securely in my palm.

"You think you can't have what you saw, but you *can*. No one can take it from you anymore."

I laugh quietly to myself. "You're supposed to have the worst trauma and darkest thoughts of all the others, yet here you are, kind of sounding like Nala right now."

"I'm kind of tired of being in the dark, to be honest. Like you've been saying, keeping things from you doesn't protect you like it used to; it just keeps you from being able to move on."

"You make it sound so easy, though. How am I supposed to move on and have that beautiful life I've always wanted, if the others still think they need to protect me?"

"I think they'd be convinced now, after today. If it convinced me, it'd convince them."

I think maybe they'd be convinced, too, but that could just be wishful thinking, and I can't get my hopes up. Either way, I'm ecstatic that I at least have Leo to understand me now.

I'm almost around the block and the house comes back into sight. Ashley and the woman are handing each other their phones, probably to exchange phone numbers. They still seem to be deep in conversation. Ashley flips her long, red hair out of her face and I feel as if my heart skips a beat.

"Okay," I hear Nala's voice say, "I'd say you've just made a major breakthrough in progress. Seems like a great time to tell Ashley how you feel now."

"What? No!" I say simply, at the ridiculous thought.

"You *did* say you were going to wait until you started making progress in therapy," Paul comments hesitantly, "so what are you waiting for now?"

"It's not progress if you guys aren't convinced you need to leave me alone more often."

They really can't be serious. Maybe it was Leo who was holding them back, so that he could talk to me privately. But if he wasn't, and they chose to come out for *this*, after everything today, then I might just lose my mind.

"Whoa, whoa," Luke says, in his usual offended tone, "whoever said anything about leaving you alone? I believe you were trying to convince us to stop trying to protect you so much, not *abandon* you."

I roll my eyes.

"Yeah," Paul agrees, "we're not abandoning you, we're just changing up our roles a bit now."

"Are you guys *really?"* I say, skeptically.

"Yes, really," Nala confirms. "We're aware of what happened. I want you to be able to have that life you've always wanted one day. We all do, okay?"

I sigh, hoping they all mean it.

I make it back to the driveway of my old house, still holding the buttercups, but this time I'm not afraid of having them taken from me.

Ashley's face lights up sweetly at the sight of me. "Hey," she says, standing up, "I was just about to go look for you." She takes a step forward and pulls me in for a tight, comforting hug. When she releases, she looks at me with those hazel eyes again. "Are you okay? You feel ready to go?"

I nod. "Yeah," I say, with a small smile.

We both turn to the woman who owns my childhood house. She stands, giving Ashley a hug then shaking my hand sincerely. Ashley mentions something about texting her for lunch next week, while I give her multiple *thank yous* for her compassion and understanding. As we walk back to the car, Ashley takes my arm again, although this time I'm not about to collapse.

"Do you think this helped you?" she asks.

"Better than I ever thought," I say, honestly.

She smiles and squeezes my arm. "I'm glad."

I suddenly feel awkward for a moment, as if I should be holding her hand, rather than just letting her hold my arm. Is this a hint? Does she want me to take her hand if she's holding my arm? Is it the right time? I don't give myself any more time to overthink it. I grab her hand and hold it in mine. She doesn't pull away; she holds mine back as we continue to walk. I sigh with relief, feeling that I can now relax better.

The air feels so fresh, so vibrant, and I breathe it in.

A few months later.

Ashley

I've known Theo for years, and it sure did take him long enough to realize that I saw him as potentially more than a friend. He finally took the hint a few months ago, grabbed my hand and held it for the first time – and I couldn't have been happier, especially on top of everything else that had happened that day. I made a new friend in probably one of the strangest ways possible, and Theo made great progress in managing his disorder, thanks to Dr. Cassidy's help and visiting his old house.

It's been a few months since that day, and Theo and I are now officially dating. Finally!

He seems happier, too; more alive and less worried. I've known him long enough to tell that he's been switching less, too, but he tells me the others always seem to still be around – they are just less argumentative and annoying now. They're there for him more in ways that he needs them to be now, supportive rather than protective.

He's told me about the talks they've had. I know most people would probably be freaked out to hear that from their partner, but I know Theo. He's not crazy or insane, and not even as much to deal with as he thinks he is. He's Theo, the guy who's had a past a little more horrible than most and, because of that, he has a defense mechanism a little more extreme than most.

Theo joins me on the couch in his apartment and puts his arm around me, as we watch a show we've recently gotten into together. I look up at him and study his face as he watches the T.V. I'm always finding myself wondering what's going on in his mind, wondering what he's thinking, and imagining how chaotic it must get in there sometimes.

"I'm thinking that you should stop staring at me and watch the show," Theo says before I can say anything, without taking his eyes off the T.V. He's used to me doing this by now.

I laugh and pull him closer to me. "I just like knowing what's going on in your mind."

He smiles and shakes his head. “Luke says you’re being weird and annoying.”

“Well, I’m not staring at Luke, so he can shut up,” I smile.

I sure don’t miss who Luke used to be. *He* was the annoying one, always causing such a hard time for Theo and loving to cause trouble. Now he’s a great guy to have whenever Theo needs to stand up and defend himself – and he would definitely have Theo’s back if Theo ever got himself into a physical fight. It’s nice to know that Theo has that sort of backup always around and ready – an advantage other people don’t have.

As for the others, they never seemed to be nearly as catastrophic as Luke was before, in my opinion. And they certainly seem to have improved their roles as well, according to what Theo has told me.

Nala has been working on not being overly positive, and accepting things as they are; accepting that sometimes it’s okay if Theo’s upset, and trying to cheer him up isn’t always the answer. It’s good to just allow people to be sad sometimes, rather than trying to constantly twist tragic circumstances into something positive.

Paul used to absolutely coddle Theo, the same as when he was a kid and Paul constantly stressed about keeping him comfortable, and as far away from uncomfortable situations as possible. Now he helps Theo through those uncomfortable situations, rather than pushing him away from them.

Then there's Leo, the brick wall; the quiet one, never trusting of anyone. He still doesn't talk much, according to Theo, and I've never seen him come out, except for that day at the house, but Theo has assured me that he communicates now. He no longer shuts himself out like he used to. When it's just him and Theo now, he understands the importance of opening up.

None of these previous roles were really a bad thing, but they aren't what Theo needs anymore. People need to grow and, in order for people to grow, things around them need to grow as well; things need to change. If the things in our life don't change with us, then our growth will be stunted.

We can end up stagnant and withering, trampled and held back from that beautiful, healthy life we've always wanted.

Theo had been held back long enough, and it was time for a change.

I look back up at him, seeing a gentle, slight smile on his face. It used to be a rare sight, seeing Theo smile, but now a simple moment like this can do it. My eyes drift to the bouquet of buttercups sitting on the side table next to us. Theo picked them for me yesterday, when he saw them outside the apartment building – a move which was *definitely* Nala's idea.

"I like my buttercups," I say, for probably the twentieth random time today.

He laughs. "Good," he says, simply.

I reach over him, pick up the small vase and hold it in front of me, gently turning it in my hands to admire the bright yellow bouquet.

Buttercups are beautiful, vibrant, yellow flowers, and just one can light up an entire room. But they're also small, dainty and delicate. When separated and seen as a lone flower, they're not nearly as beautiful or bright as when they're put together, into a bouquet. Together they're brighter, more vibrant and even healthier – better for the flowers to grow.

"You're going to spill the water if you keep playing with the vase," Theo says.

"I'm not playing with it; I'm admiring it," I say. "That's what you do when someone gives you flowers."

He smiles, watching me turn the vase to see all of the buttercups. He hugs me tightly and kisses me on my head, then laughs quietly to himself.

"What?" I say.

"I've just never known someone appreciate buttercups so much," he says.

"Well, get used to it," I say, as I reach over and carefully place the flowers back on the table.

I watch the T.V. until I realize that Theo is now staring at me.

"What?" I say again.

"Nothing," he says simply. "It's just that my head is

relaxed and quiet; no one's arguing; you're here and I'm just… happy."

I smile. "Good. Me, too."

Who would have thought that better communication would mean *less* talking, less noise and more quiet? More peace?

We pull each other closer and watch our show, both of our heads quiet and peaceful.

Thank you for reading **The Waiting Room.**

IT'S NOT A GHOST

(sneak peek)

Annika Galloway

It Doesn't Matter

Will, age 22

Present day

The waiting room is crowded today. There's too many people here and it makes me want to go insane.

Well… that's poor wording on my part; according to this world I'm already insane.

I've come alone today, as I usually do. I don't have a close family or any friends really, so I'm usually alone wherever I go, and the waiting room is not an exception.

Being here seems so pointless, yet here I am, just going where I'm told to go, for no reason that will benefit me personally. Who will it benefit then, you may ask?

This hospital, for taking a $50 co-pay from me on top of my family's already poor insurance, my family who will feel better that I'm "getting help" for my "disorder," and we can't forget my therapist, who gets to brag about how cool his patient's case is without actually using my real name because talking about me is breaking confidentiality for him, though I couldn't care less about confidentiality. I couldn't care less who knows what goes on in my head. None of this matters anyway.

My name is Will Dodson and I'm 22 years old, though that information doesn't matter. What matters here is what my so-called "disorder" is and why I'm here today in this crowded, stuffy waiting room.

Actually, on second thought, that doesn't matter either. Nothing matters here. It doesn't matter that the old woman sitting a few chairs away from me seems upset. It doesn't matter that the receptionist at the counter looked too stressed to greet me as I walked in earlier. It doesn't matter that the girl sitting across the waiting room from me is getting into an argument with her brother. It doesn't matter that a few of the obnoxious fluorescent lights in the ceiling are out. It doesn't matter here.

Nothing matters here.

"Stacy," A doctor steps through one of the doors of the waiting room and calls out a last name. A woman stands and gathers her things from her worn down waiting room chair. She looks exhausted, as if she's just about ready to give up on absolutely everything right here in this waiting room.

I feel that energy, but I guess for me, it's in a more angry tone rather than depressed.

The lady makes her way through the door as the doctor holds it open for her. "How are we feeling today?" the doctor asks, as their footsteps fade away and the door closes.

We. I hate when people do that. I have yet to meet another person who feels the same as me, who has the same "disorder" as me, but with why I'm here, it's quite literally impossible for another human in this world to feel how I feel and think how I think. This world is just too small.

In the first session I had with my therapist here, he

did the same thing that obnoxious doctor just did to that woman. He asked, "So, how are we feeling today?"

"We" responded with "*We* feel like our lives, families, kids, wives or husbands or whatever you love is completely pointless and so is this session." He hasn't asked how "we" were feeling since. Now he asks how I, myself, am doing and no one else.

"Therapist," I said in our last session (I refuse to learn his name. It makes him more humanized), "You realize none of this matters, right?"

"You ask me that every time, Will," Therapist said, "my answer hasn't changed. I still agree to disagree with you there. My family matters, my job, house, you. You matter, though I know you don't believe that. But like I've said, that's what we're, I mean *you're* here to work on." He's getting a bit smarter. He caught himself trying to unite us and make us look like buddies by using "we" again.

"The only reason I'm here is because I have to be here," I said.

"And what exactly is making you be here?" He asked.

I stayed silent and gave him a death glare.

"Oh right," Therapist said, "I forgot you don't like when we start to make progress. Should I just ask you what your favorite ice cream flavor is instead? You like talking about how things are pointless, maybe you might like answering pointless questions."

"Ice cream doesn't matter," I responded.

"Then which flavor doesn't matter the most?"

He's getting good, I'll give him that. He's started to catch up on the tone I usually use, which involves a lot of not caring what someone else thinks, so usually a heavy amount of smartassery and sarcasm.

"Cherry ice cream," I said.

"So that's the worst kind of ice cream?"

"Without a doubt."

I jump at the sudden voice breaking me out of my thoughts.

"Is this seat taken?" A man probably somewhere also in his twenties asks. I look up and unfortunately he's talking to me.

"It doesn't matter," I say flatly and turn my head in the opposite direction, to make sure he doesn't think I'm inviting him into any conversation.

"If someone's sitting here, it's alright. I can find another."

I sigh. *So annoying*. "No one's sitting there."

The man hesitates, then awkwardly sits next to me.

We're silent, my favorite kind of conversation. I glance over at him and I can already tell what kind of person he is: a talking kind.

Don't do it, I think to myself. He wants to talk, I just know it. He's the kind of guy who thinks all silences have to be awkward, when in reality most of them are rather peaceful.

I turn from him, but I can feel his eyes drift towards me.

Don't do it, don't do it, don't do it, don't—

"So," he says.

Damn it.

"It's crowded here today, isn't it?"

I nod, "Yep."

"Have you been here before? 'Cause this waiting room seems to get sadder with every visit." He laughs to himself.

"Been here plenty of times. It sucks."

The guy laughs. "You'd think they could at least get some better chairs."

I turned to him. "Alright man, I'm really not into small talk, or honestly really any kind of talking. So you really don't have to…" I gesture with my hand, "do this."

He's quiet for a moment, probably feeling that heaviness in the air most people feel that I don't.

"Ah," he says, "I take it you probably didn't want me sitting here after all."

"Nothing personal," I say, "I just don't want to be here, and talking about being here only reminds me that I'm here. So let's just not."

"Someone making you be here?" he asks. Obviously, his curiosity is taking over now. *Great, he'll never shut up now.*

"You could say that," I say.

"But no one's with you here?"

"It doesn't matter." Whatever reason this guy is here for, it must be because of some talking disorder I don't know about. I mean, come on, normal people don't talk to each other in waiting rooms, especially hospital waiting rooms, and especially – *especially* psychiatric hospital/therapy waiting rooms.

"Ah," he says simply. I can tell he wants to ask more, but the fear that getting too personal is socially unacceptable is stopping him. That and also probably how cold and closed off I'm being.

"Well, sorry for talking more than you prefer," he says, "I'm just alone here too, and the atmosphere here is so depressing. Helps me personally to be able to talk, even if it's to a random stranger."

A random stranger. There's tons of those in this waiting room and he really had to go with choosing me, probably the most closed off random stranger in this entire room, entire world perhaps.

"Aren't you here to talk to a professional though?" I ask, but not looking for an answer, more like just to remind him that he's here to talk to someone that's not me, so he can stop talking to me and leave me alone now.

"Yeah, yeah I am," he says.

That seemed to finally end the conversation, and I can tell I've made the poor guy feel like an awkward mess internally as he sits quietly now, biting his lower lip. There's no telling what overthinking mess is recklessly thrashing its way through his head right now.

I'd feel bad if I believed he actually existed.

End of sneak peek...

ABOUT THE AUTHOR

Annika Galloway (pronounced Anna-ka) was born and raised in Birmingham, Alabama, except for the time when she lived in Siem Reap, Cambodia as a teenager for a short while. During her time there, she learned a lot about mental wellbeing, as well as physical. She is now a major in psychology, so that she can better understand perspectives different from her own and incorporate what she studies into her books. She writes her books hoping to inspire her readers and show them these different perspectives, reminding them that everyone has their own struggles, and that's okay.

Visit Annika Galloway at annikagallowayauthor.com or follow her on Instagram for the latest updates: @annikagallowaybooks

More books by Annika Galloway coming soon.

Thank you for reading.

Don't forget to check Annika Galloway's previous book,

The Happy Treatment

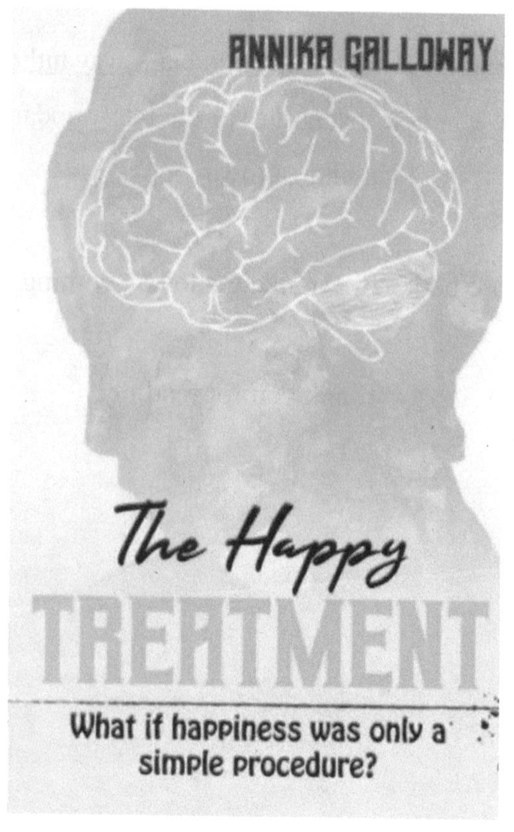

WHAT IF HAPPINESS WAS ONLY A SIMPLE PROCEDURE?

www.ingramcontent.com/pod-product-compliance
Ingram Content Group UK Ltd.
Pitfield, Milton Keynes, MK11 3LW, UK
UKHW012250290726
14090UKWH00016B/564

9 798218 329396